# FAITH & WORD EDITION
# BLEST ARE WE

*Faith comes from what is heard,*
*and what is heard comes through the word of Christ.*

Romans 10:17

## Series Authors

Rev. Richard N. Fragomeni, Ph.D.
Maureen Gallagher, Ph.D.
Jeannine Goggin, M.P.S.
Michael P. Horan, Ph.D.

### Scripture Co-editor and Consultant
Maria Pascuzzi, S.S.L., S.T.D.

### Multicultural Consultant
Angela Erevia, M.C.D.P., M.R.E.

**Silver Burdett Ginn Religion**
A Scott Foresman Imprint
Parsippany, NJ

# BLEST ARE WE

## Contributing Writers

Janie Gustafson, Ph.D.
*Family Time Scripture:* Michael J. Williams, M.S.
*Feasts and Seasons:* Marianne K. Lenihan
*Our Catholic Heritage:* Patricia Enwright

## Advisory Board

William C. Allegri, M.A., Patricia M. Feeley, S.S.J., M.A.,
Edmund F. Gordon, Patricia A. Hoffmann, Cris V.
Villapando, D.Min.

## Consultants

Margaret J. Borders, M.R.S., Kelly O'Lague Dulka,
M.S.W., Diane Hardick, M.A., Debra Schurko,
Linda S. Tonelli, M.Ed., Joy Villotti-Biedrzycki

## Music Advisor

*GIA Publications:* Michael A. Cymbala, Alec Harris,
Robert W. Piercy

## Nihil Obstat

M. Kathleen Flanagan, S.C., Ph.D.
Censor Librorum

## Imprimatur

✠Most Reverend Arthur J. Serratelli
Bishop of Paterson
April 25, 2006

The *nihil* obstat and *imprimatur* are official declarations that a book
or pamphlet is free of doctrinal and moral error. No implication is
contained therein that those who have granted the *nihil obstat* and
*imprimatur* agree with the contents, opinions, or statements expressed.

## Acknowledgments

Excerpts from *The New American Bible* © 1970 by the Confraternity
of Christian Doctrine, Washington, DC, including *The Revised New
Testament* © 1986 by the Confraternity of Christian Doctrine,
Washington, DC, used with permission. All rights reserved.

All adaptations of Scripture are based on *The New American Bible*
© 1970 and 1986.

Excerpts from the English translation of *Rite of Penance* © 1974,
ICEL; excerpts from the English translation of *Eucharistic Prayers
for Masses with Children* © 1975, ICEL; excerpts from the English
translation of *The Roman Missal, Second Edition* © 1973, ICEL. All
rights reserved.

Music selections copyrighted and/or administered by GIA Publications
are used with permission of GIA Publications, Inc., 7404 So. Mason
Avenue, Chicago, IL 60638-9927. Please refer to songs for specific
copyright dates and information.

"Thumb Prayer" adapted from *Catechist* magazine. © Page McKean
Zyromski, contributing editor.

*In Appreciation:* Blessed Kateri Church, Sparta, NJ; Blessed Sacrament
Church, Newark, NJ; Church of the Assumption, Morristown, NJ; Our
Lady of Mercy Church, Whippany, NJ; Our Lady of the Lake Church,
Sparta, NJ; St. Ann's Church, Parsippany, NJ; St. Joseph's Church,
Croton Falls, NY; St. Peter the Apostle Church, Parsippany, NJ;
St. Thomas More Church, Convent Station, NJ; GIA Publications, Inc.,
Chicago, IL; WLP Publications, Franklin Park, IL; Rev. George Hafemann

## Credits

**COVER:** Gene Plaisted, OSC/The Crosiers

**LET US PRAY ART:** 9, 12, 13 Jill Dubin; 15 Beth Foster Wiggins

**SCRIPTURE ART:** Diane Paterson

**ALL OTHER ART:** 9–16 Maria Jimenez; 17–19, 26–28, 46, 48, 56, 58,
68, 70, 75, 78, 90, 98, 100, 110, 112, 120, 122, 130, 132, 140, 142,
152, 154, 162, 172, 174, 184, 194, 196, 214, 216, 224, 226, 252, 253,
258 Diane Paterson; 20, 21 Elizabeth Wolf; 31, 34 Nan Brooks; 33 Marion
Eldridge; 37, 76, 111, 257 Judy Stead; 37 Diana Magnuson; 41 Ginna
Magee; 43 John Hovell; 44, 85, 159, 212, 246, 247 Bernadette Lau;
50 Masami Miyamoto; 51, 103 Laura Huliska-Beith; 57 Melinda Levine;
61–64, 239 Lyn Martin; 67, 82, 205, 249 Morella Fuenmayor; 69 George
Ulrich; 72, 134, 156, 245 Dorothy Stott; 73 Karen Bell; 79, 163, 173, 183
Randy Chewning; 93 Jean & Mou-Sien Tseng; 99 Paige Billin-Frye; 106,
128 Heather Graham; 115, 219 Tom Sperling; 118, 148 Julie Monks; 127
Anne Stanley; 131, 141 George Hamblin; 131 Barb Massey; 134, 156
Roman Dunets; 138, 169 Shelley Dieterichs; 145 Linda Howard Bittner;
145 Patti Green; 147 Michael Di Giorgio; 167 David Austin Clar; 177
Lauren Cryan; 182 Tim Ladwig; 187, 225 Pat Hoggan; 190, 198 Jill Dubin;
209 Gregg Valley; 215 Donna Perrone; 229 Sandy Rabinowitz; 232 Marcie
Hawthorne; 234 Phyllis Pollema-Cahill; 240 Linda Weller; 241 David
Bathurst; 243 Kathleen Kuchera; 247 Cindy Rosenheim

**PHOTOS:** Every effort has been made to secure permission and provide
appropriate credit for photographic material. The publisher deeply regrets
any omission and pledges to correct errors called to its attention in
subsequent editions.Unless otherwise acknowledged, all photographs are
the property of Scott Foresman, a division of Pearson Education.
6 Myrleen Ferguson Cate/PhotoEdit; 7 Gene Plaisted, OSC/The Crosiers;
23 (Bkgd) © The Israel Museum, Jerusalem, (Inset) Jim Whitmer; 26 (BL)
Gene Plaisted, OSC/The Crosiers, (B) Michael St. Maur Sheil/Corbis; 27
Michael Newman/PhotoEdit, (T) Paul Barton/Corbis; 36 © W.P. Wittman, (B)
National Gallery, London/Photograph by Erich Lessing/Art Resource, NY;
47 (TR) Vince Streano/Corbis, (L) Kwame Zikomo/SuperStock, (BR) Myrleen
Ferguson Cate/PhotoEdit; 52 ©Donald Nausbaum/Stone; 62 Pablo Coral/
Corbis; 65 Z. Radovan, Jerusalem; 68 Hermitage Museum, St. Petersburg,
Russia/Bridgeman Art Library, London/SuperStock; 74 ©Tim Brown/
Stone; 78 Corbis Sygma; 84 Fotopic/Omni-Photo Communications, Inc.;
88 (B) Aaron Rapoport/Castle Rock Entertainment/The Kobal Collection,
(B) Bibliotheque Municipale, Dijon, France/Giraudon/Art Resource, NY,
(T) ©Jon Arnold/Alamy Images; 94 Adam Woolfitt/Woodfin Camp &
Associates/PictureQuest; 98 Everett Collection, Inc.; 104 CLEO; 107 (Bkgd)
Barry Searle/©Sonia Halliday Photographs, (Inset) James L. Shaffer/Editorial
Development Associates; 110 Newberry Library, Chicago/SuperStock; 114
Sisters of Providence White Violet Center for Eco Justice; 116 © Robert
Fried; 120 Macduff Everton/Corbis; 121 ©Lawrence Migdale/Stone; 124
©Bill Wittman; 126 Paul Conklin/PhotoEdit; 130 Pennsylvania Department
of Conservation & Natural Resources; 136 (Inset) Bettmann/Corbis, (Bkgd)
Danilo G. Donadoni/Bruce Coleman Inc.; 140 Gene Plaisted, OSC/The
Crosiers; 144 (T) Index Stock Imagery, (B) Peterson/Getty Images; 146
Earth Imaging/Stone; 149 (Bkgd) Z. Radovan, Jerusalem, (Inset) © Tony
Freeman/PhotoEdit/PictureQuest; 150 Myrleen Ferguson Cate/PhotoEdit;
158 Tony Freeman/PhotoEdit; 161 Felicia Martinez/PhotoEdit; 162
Bettmann/Corbis; 164 Myrleen Ferguson Cate/PhotoEdit; 172 Catholic
News Service; 181 Milt & Joan Mann/Cameramann International, Ltd.;
182 Museo dell'Opera Metropolitana, Siena, Italy/Scala/Art Resource,
NY; 186 PhotoEdit; 188 (L) John Gerlach/TOM STACK & ASSOCIATES,
(R) C.P. George/Visuals Unlimited; 191 (Bkgd) David Lees/Corbis, (Inset)
Michael Newman/PhotoEdit; 194 Rasmussen/Sipa Press; 195 (L) Catherine
Karnow/Woodfin Camp & Associates, (TR) E. Crews/Image Works; 198 Don
Smetzer/Stone; 200 Peter Cade/Stone; 204 (T) Gene Plaisted, OSC/The
Crosiers, (B) Courtesy, Little Sisters of the Poor; 206 Gene Plaisted, OSC/
The Crosiers; 208 ©Alessandra Benedetti/Corbis; 210 Michael Gadomski/
Animals Animals/Earth Scenes; 214 Michael Newman/PhotoEdit; 218 (TL)
Lori Grinker/Contact Press Images, (TR) Charles Caratini/Corbis Sygma,
(BL) Lawrence, Migdale/Stock, Boston/PictureQuest, (BR) Daemmrich
Photography; 220 © David Tejada; 228 (TR) Robert Brenner/PhotoEdit,
(L) Myrleen Ferguson Cate/PhotoEdit; 233 Ariel Skelley/Corbis; 238 Jan Stromme/
PhotoEdit, Alinari/Regione Umbria/Art Resource, NY; 242 © David
Madison/Getty Images/Stone; 244 Jack Kurtz; 248 SuperStock; 250 James
L. Shaffer; 256 Our Lady of Victory; 259 The Pierpont Morgan Library/Art
Resource, NY; 262 © W.P. Wittman; 263 (TC) MacDonald Photography/
Unicorn Stock Photos, (B) Bob Daemmrich/Image Works, (BC) © W.P.
Wittman; 264 Gene Plaisted, OSC/The Crosiers; 271 (B) Myrleen Ferguson
Cate/PhotoEdit, (T) The Pierpont Morgan Library/Art Resource, NY; 274
CLEO; 276 (B) Bob Daemmrich/Stock, Boston/PictureQuest, (T) Myrleen
Ferguson Cate/PhotoEdit

1 2 3 4 5 6 7 8 9 10 – V003 – 16 15 14 13 12 11 10 09 08 07 06

# CONTENTS

WHAT CATHOLICS BELIEVE

HOW CATHOLICS WORSHIP

HOW CATHOLICS LIVE

HOW CATHOLICS PRAY

4

WHAT CATHOLICS BELIEVE

HOW CATHOLICS WORSHIP

HOW CATHOLICS LIVE

HOW CATHOLICS PRAY

WHAT CATHOLICS BELIEVE

HOW CATHOLICS WORSHIP

HOW CATHOLICS LIVE

HOW CATHOLICS PRAY

# FEASTS AND SEASONS

# OUR CATHOLIC HERITAGE

*Organized according to the 4 pillars of the Catechism*

# LET US PRAY

# The Sign of the Cross

In the name of the Father
and of the Son
and of the Holy Spirit.
Amen.

# The Hail Mary

Hail, Mary, full of grace,
the Lord is with thee.
Blessed art thou among
women
and blessed is the fruit
of thy womb, Jesus.
Holy Mary, Mother of God,
pray for us sinners,
now and at the hour
of our death.
Amen.

# The Lord's Prayer

Our Father
   who art in heaven,
   hallowed be thy name.
Thy kingdom come.
Thy will be done on earth,
   as it is in heaven.
Give us this day
   our daily bread,
and forgive us our trespasses,
   as we forgive those
   who trespass against us,
and lead us not
   into temptation,
   but deliver us from evil.
Amen.

# Padre Nuestro

Padre nuestro,
   que estás en el cielo,
   santificado sea tu Nombre;
venga a nosotros tu reino;
hágase tu voluntad en la tierra
   como en el cielo.
Danos hoy nuestro
   pan de cada día;
perdona nuestras ofensas,
   como también nosotros
   perdonamos
   a los que nos ofenden;
no nos dejes caer en la tentación,
   y líbranos del mal.
Amén.

# The Nicene Creed

We believe in one God, the Father, the Almighty,
    maker of heaven and earth,
    of all that is, seen and unseen.

We believe in one Lord, Jesus Christ,
    the only Son of God, eternally begotten of the Father,
    God from God, Light from Light,
    true God from true God, begotten, not made,
    one in Being with the Father.
    Through Him all things were made.
    For us men and for our salvation
        He came down from heaven:
    by the power of the Holy Spirit
    He was born of the Virgin Mary, and became Man.

For our sake He was crucified under Pontius Pilate;
    He suffered, died, and was buried.

On the third day He rose again
    in fulfillment of the Scriptures;
    He ascended into heaven,
    and is seated at the right hand of the Father.

He will come again in glory to judge the living and the dead,
    and His kingdom will have no end.

We believe in the Holy Spirit, the Lord, the Giver of life,
    Who proceeds from the Father and the Son.
    With the Father and the Son He is worshiped and glorified.
    He has spoken through the prophets.
    We believe in one, holy, catholic, and apostolic Church.
    We acknowledge one Baptism for the forgiveness of sins.
    We look for the resurrection of the dead,
        and the life of the world to come.
Amen.

# Glory Be to the Father

Glory be to the Father
    and to the Son
    and to the Holy Spirit,
as it was in the beginning
    is now, and ever shall be
    world without end.
Amen.

# Prayer to the Holy Spirit

Come, Holy Spirit,
    renew the hearts of thy faithful
    and kindle in them
    the fire of thy love.
Send forth thy Spirit,
    and they shall be created;
and thou shalt renew
    the face of the earth.
Amen.

# Morning Prayer

Loving God, bless the work we do.
Watch over us and guide us in
school and at home.
Help us realize that everything
we do gives praise to you.
We make this prayer in
Jesus' name.
Amen.

# Evening Prayer

*Parent:*    May God bless you and keep you.

*Child:*    May he guide us in life.

*Parent:*    May he bless you this evening.

*Child:*    And keep us in his sight.

*Parent:*    May God be with you, (name).

*Child:*    And also with you.

*Together:*    In the name of the Father, and of the Son, and of the Holy Spirit. Amen.

# Angel of God

Angel of God, my guardian dear,
  to whom God's love commits me here,
ever this day be at my side,
  to light and guard, to rule and guide.
Amen.

# Prayer of Sorrow

My God,
  I am sorry for my sins with all my heart.
In choosing to do wrong
  and failing to do good,
  I have sinned against you
  whom I should love above all things.
I firmly intend, with your help,
  to do penance, to sin no more,
  and to avoid whatever leads me to sin.
Our Savior Jesus Christ
  suffered and died for us.
  In his name, my God, have mercy.
Amen.

*Rite of Penance*

# Grace *Before* Meals

Bless us, O Lord,
and these thy gifts,
which we are about to
receive
from thy bounty,
through Christ our Lord.
Amen.

# Grace *After* Meals

We give thee thanks for all thy gifts,
almighty God,
living and reigning now and forever.
Amen.

## My Prayer *to* Jesus *in the* Eucharist

Amen.

# The Bible

**Blessed are those who hear
the Word of God and obey it.**

Based on Luke 11:28

# The Bible

The Bible is the Word of God. This holy book helps us learn about God's great love for us. Many people wrote Bible stories. The Holy Spirit guided all writers of the Bible.

     The Bible is also called **Scripture.** There are readings from Scripture at Mass.

## Old Testament

The Old Testament has stories about people who lived on earth before Jesus. It tells the story of creation. It tells about Moses and the commandments.

## New Testament

The New Testament tells about the life and teachings of Jesus. It begins with a **Gospel**. Gospel means "good news." There are four Gospels. They are named for four followers of Jesus — Matthew, Mark, Luke, and John.

The Bible teaches us how to act as children of God.

# Activity

What story do you remember from the Bible?
Write or draw a picture about it.

# The Life of Jesus

**Bethlehem**  **wise men**  **Nazareth** **Temple** **fishermen**  **cross**

Jesus was born in  .

 went to Bethlehem to see Jesus.

Jesus grew up in  .

At Jerusalem, Jesus taught in the  .

Jesus asked  to follow him.

Jesus died on the  near Jerusalem.

Look at the map on the next page. It shows places where Jesus lived and taught.

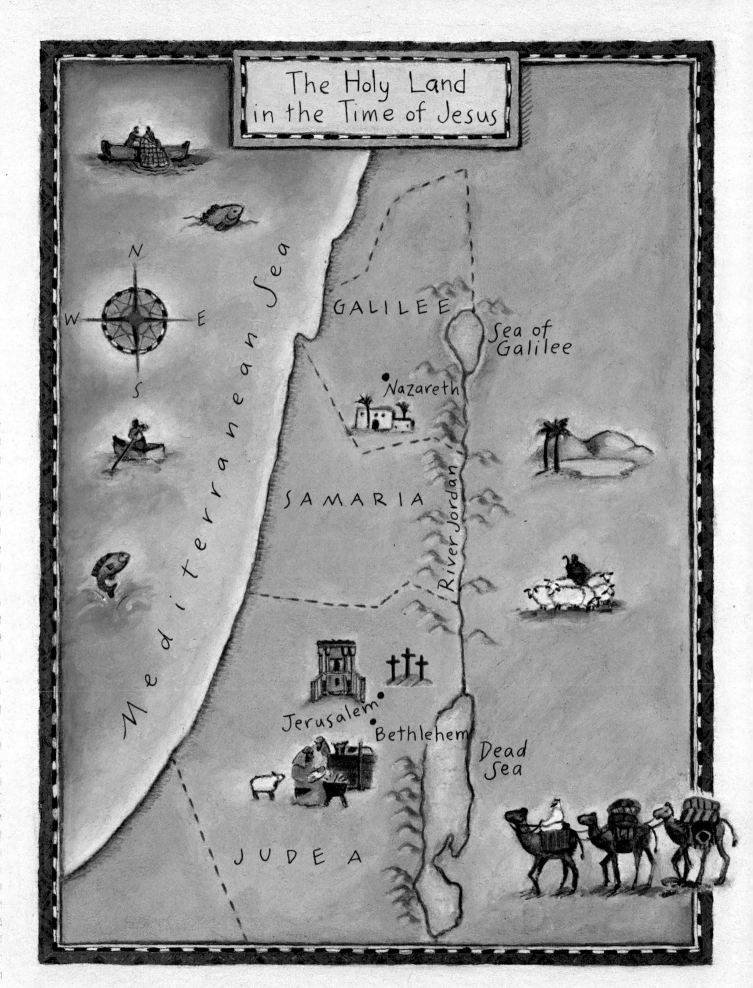

The Holy Land
in the Time of Jesus

N
W    E
S

Mediterranean Sea

GALILEE

Sea of Galilee

Nazareth

SAMARIA

River Jordan

JUDEA

Jerusalem

Bethlehem

Dead Sea

# BLEST ARE WE

Words and Music by David Haas
Spanish translation by Ronald F. Krisman

**REFRAIN**

Blest are we, ho - ly chil - dren of light— are— we!
¡Ben - de - ci - dos, so - mos san - tos hi - jos de la luz!

Blest are we, cho - sen peo - ple of God!
¡Ben - de - ci - dos y e - le - gi - dos por Dios!

Blest are we, God has plans— for you and me!
¡Ben - de - ci - dos, Dios nos quie - re ser cual Je - sús!

*Fine*

Blest— are we!— We are the chil - dren of God!
¡Ben - de - ci - dos, so - mos los hi - jos de Dios!

**VERSE**

1. For our world,— each sis - ter and broth - er:
1. Por el mun - do, por to - dos sus pue - blos:

We are called,— called to serve!—
¡So - mos lla - ma - dos pa - ra ser - vir!

We are here to love— one an - oth - er:
Nos a - me - mos los u - nos a los o - tros;—

*D.C.*

We— are called, called— to serve!—
¡So - mos lla - ma - dos pa - ra ser - vir!—

2. For the poor, the meek and the lowly:
We are called, called to serve!
For the weak, the sick and the hungry:
We are called, called to serve!

3. For all those who yearn for freedom:
We are called, called to serve!
For the world, to be God's kingdom:
We are called, called to serve!

2. Por los pobres, los mansos y humildes:
¡Somos llamados para servir!
Por los enfermos, hambrientos, y débiles:
¡Somos llamados para servir!

3. Por los que sufren y quieren ser librados:
¡Somos llamados paraservir!
Venga a nosotros el Reino de los Cielos:
¡Somos llamados paraservir!

# We Gather as Believers

Our parish church community comes together each week. We give praise and thanks to God and we celebrate our faith.

*It is good to give thanks to the LORD,*
*to sing praise to your name, Most High.*
Psalm 92:2

King David gave thanks to God through joyful song. We gather in church to sing our praise and thanks to God.

# You Have Put On Christ

*Music by Howard Hughes*

*Cantor, then All*

You— have— put on Christ, in him you have been bap - tized.

Al - le - lu - ia, al - le - lu - ia.

# Take Home

FAMILY TIME

## Our Church Welcomes Us

The chapters in Unit 1 focus on membership in the Catholic Church. This first chapter explains being welcomed into the community of believers and being a small part of something larger.

### ACTIVITY

**Plant a Vine**  Together, plant a vine, such as ivy, in a flowerpot, or buy one already planted. Help your child name the parts of the plant (roots, stems, and leaves) and then share that these small parts make up the whole plant.

## WEEKLY PLANNER

### On Sunday
Show hospitality to others. As you go into church, greet the people around you and make them feel welcome.

### On the Web
**www.blestarewe.com**

 Visit our Web site for the saint of the day and the reflection question of the week.

### Saint of the Week

 **Saint Matthew**
**(first century)**

Saint Matthew was an apostle of Jesus and a gospel writer. When Jesus asked Matthew, known as Levi, to follow him, Matthew left his job as a tax collector to do so.

**Patron Saint of:** accountants and bankers
**Feast Day:** September 21

A Prayer for the Week

O God, we ask that we may be open to others, welcoming them into our Church. Help us to learn from Saint Matthew how to follow you. Amen.

# Getting ready for Chapter 1

# Take Home

FAMILY TIME

## ✝ Scripture Background

### In and Before the Time of Jesus

**Houses** Many Israelite houses had four rooms. Some featured one room the width of the house with three long rooms stemming from it. Houses that were two stories high had outside stairs to the second floor. The flat roofs were often made of branches mixed with mud or straw. In hot weather, people slept on the roofs. They also dried fruit and grain on them. Since Levi was a wealthy man, his house may have been larger and, possibly, more ornate.

You can read about Levi in Luke 7:27–32.

# OUR CATHOLIC TRADITION in Design

**Altar Tables** In the early Church the Eucharist was celebrated around a table, usually as a shared meal. During the great persecutions, the Eucharist was often celebrated using the tombs of the martyrs as altar tables.

During the Middle Ages, permanent altars became quite ornate and eventually looked more like monuments than tables for a sacred meal.

Inspired by the Second Vatican Council, twentieth-century reforms in the liturgy called for the celebrant to face the community and for the altar to take the form of a table around which the People of God could gather for the eucharistic feast.

# 1 Our Church Welcomes Us

O God, you have brought us here together.
We give you thanks and praise.

Based on Eucharistic Prayer for Masses with Children I

## Share

A community is a place where people make you
feel welcome. In a family, people share life and love.
In a neighborhood, people live near each other.
In a classroom, people learn together.

What communities make you feel welcome?

_____

- - - - - - - - - - - - - - - - - - - - - - - - - - - - - -

**1.** I belong to the _____ family.

_____

- - - - - - - - - - - - - - - - - - - - - - - - - - - - - -

**2.** I belong to _____ Parish.

How is the Catholic parish a community?

# Hear & Believe

## ✠ Scripture  A Warm Welcome

One day, Jesus met a man who collected taxes. His name was Levi. Jesus asked, "Levi, will you follow me?"

"Yes," Levi answered. He was happy to become a follower of Jesus.

That night, Levi invited his friends and Jesus to a dinner in his home. Jesus was the guest of honor. Levi made all his guests feel welcome.

Based on Luke 5:27–29

## God's People

Today, we welcome others like Levi did. As followers of Jesus we are open to everyone. We are the **People of God**. We celebrate a special meal at **Mass**. It shows God's love for us.

## Our Church Teaches

Our parish is a community that worships, works, and plays together. As part of the Catholic Church, our parish welcomes all people. There is one way all the People of God are alike. We are followers of Jesus Christ. We welcome all who believe in Jesus.

### We Believe

We are the People of God. We celebrate all who believe in Jesus.

### Faith Words

**People of God**
The People of God are followers of Jesus Christ.

How do church members act?

# Respond

## Welcome, Neighbors!

Tommy and his family came to the United States to escape a war in their country. Soldiers had put them out of their home.

Father Louis and the people of St. John's Parish want to help. The family will live in a house that belongs to the Church. A teacher is helping Tommy's family learn English. Some parish families are bringing food and clothes. Others bring books and toys. Father Louis is helping Tommy's dad find a job.

**?** How do the people of St. John's Parish show that they are the People of God?

# Activities

1. In the box, draw a picture of people who are caring for others.

2. Talk about ways to make other people feel welcome.

How can we celebrate being the People of God?

# Prayer Celebration

## A Prayer of Thanksgiving

We celebrate being the
People of God by praying
together.

**Leader:** Sing with joy to God!
Be glad to serve the Lord.

**All:** We are the People of God.

**Leader:** God made us.
God calls us together
as one Church.

**All:** We are the People of God.

**Leader:** Give thanks to God, who is
always good. Be joyful, for
God's kindness lasts forever.

**All:** We are the People of God.
Amen.

Based on Psalm 100

# Chapter Review

**A** **Circle** the correct answer.

1. We _____ together as the People of God.

   **pray**          **run**          **travel**

2. Our Church _____ all people.

   **forgets**          **knows**          **welcomes**

3. The Mass celebrates God's _____ for us.

   **love**          **need**          **worry**

4. As Catholics, we are all followers of _____.

   **Jean**          **Jesus**          **John**

**B** **Write** what we are called to do as the People of God.

As the People of God, we are called to

_____

- - - - - - - - - - - - - - - - - - - - - - - - - - - - - - - - -

_____.

# Faith in Action

**Family and Community** Some families belong to a parish welcoming committee. They greet people as they come to Mass. They help new families learn about parish activities. They even help visitors to feel welcome.

## In Your Parish

**Activity** Complete this welcome badge. Make one like it to wear it as a parish greeter.

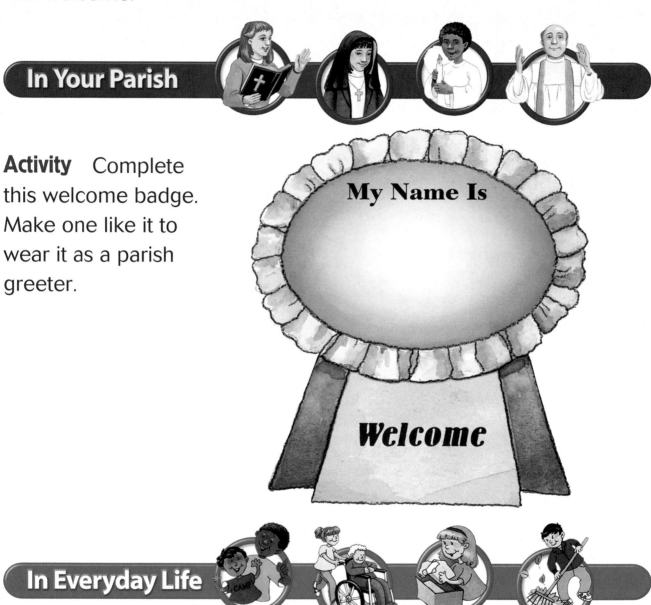

My Name Is

Welcome

## In Everyday Life

**Activity** Think about ways that you can make someone feel welcome. Share how you would do this at home, at school, or in your neighborhood.

# Take Home

FAMILY TIME

# We Belong to the Church

This chapter describes the journey your child has begun in the faith. Baptism uses common elements, such as water, light, and oil as signs of our membership in the Catholic Church.

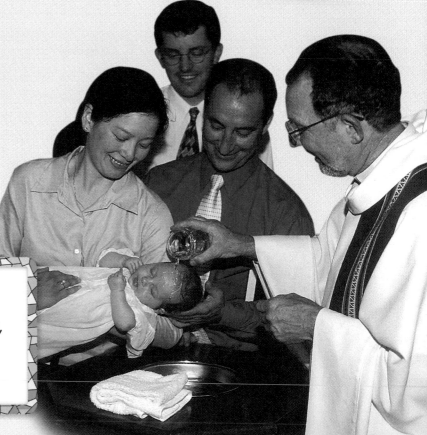

## ACTIVITY

**Signs of Baptism** Show pictures of baptisms of family members. Discuss the signs of white clothes, blessed water, oil, and a lighted candle. Share stories about the experience.

---

# WEEKLY PLANNER

## On Sunday

Upon entering church, use the holy water font and make the Sign of the Cross. Remember your membership in the Church as a follower of Jesus.

## On the Web

**www.blestarewe.com**

Visit our Web site for the saint of the day and the reflection question of the week.

## Saint of the Week

 **Saint Josephine Bakhita** (1868–1947)

As a child living in Sudan, Josephine Bakhita was sold into slavery. She was later sent to Italy. There, in 1896, she converted to Catholicism and became a religious sister.

**Patron Saint of:** Sudan
**Feast Day:** February 8

A Prayer for the Week

Jesus, we are grateful to be a part of your Church. We know that belonging to your Church will bring us happiness and blessings. Amen.

# Take Home

FAMILY TIME

## ✚ Scripture Background

### Before the Time of Jesus

**Baptism** Before its institution as a Christian sacrament, baptism was a term used to signify Jewish ritual cleansing or purification. Jewish priests performed baptisms to welcome new members. Christian baptism of converts carried on the tradition of purification for entry into the new covenant. Biblical comparisons with baptism include Israel's Exodus through the sea, Noah's salvation from the Flood, and Jesus' death and Resurrection.

You can read about purification in Genesis 7:12–23; 1 Corinthians 10:1–3.

## OUR CATHOLIC TRADITION in Art

**The Baptism of Christ** *The Baptism of Christ* by Piero della Francesca is one of the finest paintings of the Italian Renaissance. The painting is now in the National Gallery in London, but it was originally an altarpiece in the chapel of St. John the Baptist in Piero's native town, Sansepolcro, in central Italy.

The painting illustrates the artist's concept of Christ's baptism when St. John pours water from a bowl over Christ as the Holy Spirit descends from heaven.

# 2 We Belong to the Church

 We are children of the light.
We are children of the day.

Based on 1 Thessalonians 5:5

# Share

People have many ways to show they belong to a group.

Look at these pictures.
Match each sign of belonging with its group.
Then tell about a sign of belonging that you have.

| SIGN | GROUP |
|------|-------|

What signs of belonging do church members have?

# Hear & Believe

## Worship The Sacraments

Special signs help us celebrate our life in the Catholic Church. They are called **sacraments**. Sacraments are signs of God's love and presence.

The first sacrament all Catholics receive is **Baptism**. In Baptism we begin to share in Jesus' life.

The very first people God created disobeyed God. This is called **original sin**. Baptism takes away original sin and all sin. We are united with Jesus who came to forgive sins.

The Catholic Church uses four signs to help us celebrate Baptism.

1. The priest or deacon pours blessed water over the child's head. At the same time he says, "I baptize you in the name of the Father, and of the Son, and of the Holy Spirit."

2. On the child's forehead the priest or deacon makes the Sign of the Cross. He does this with blessed oil.

**3.** The child receives white clothes. The priest or deacon says, "You have become new. You have put on Christ."

**4.** The child's godparents receive a lighted candle. The priest or deacon says, "Receive the light of Christ."

Based on the Rite of Baptism for Children

## Signs of New Life

We are welcomed as members of the Church at Baptism. The special signs of Baptism remind us that we share in the life of Christ. Jesus Christ died for us and rose to new life.

## Our Church Teaches

A priest or deacon is the usual minister of Baptism. In some cases, anyone may baptize as the Church would wish using water and the words of the sacrament. Baptism takes away original sin and all sin. We become the children of God. We receive the Holy Spirit.

How can we show others we belong to the Church?

# Respond
## Bringing Light to Others

"What a great day!" thought Rita. "My twin baby brothers, Samuel and Joshua, were baptized today. Someday, I will tell them all about it. I'll tell them about the beautiful Easter candle. It reminds us that Jesus is the Light of the World.

"I will tell them about their godfather, Uncle Al. He lit two small candles from the Easter candle for them. The small candles remind us to keep the light of Jesus alive inside us. They remind us to bring Christ's light to others by our words and actions.

"Sam and Josh are already bringing light into my life!"

**?** What are some ways you can bring God's light to others?

# Activity

Use these words to complete the puzzle.

| | | |
|---|---|---|
| belonging | Light | sacrament |
| children | Water | sin |

## Down

**1.** We are all born with original _____.

**2.** Baptism is a sign of _____ to the Church.

**4.** _____ is used in Baptism.

## Across

**3.** We are _____ of God.

**5.** A _____ is a sign of God's love.

**6.** Jesus is the _____ of the World.

How can we celebrate that we are God's children?

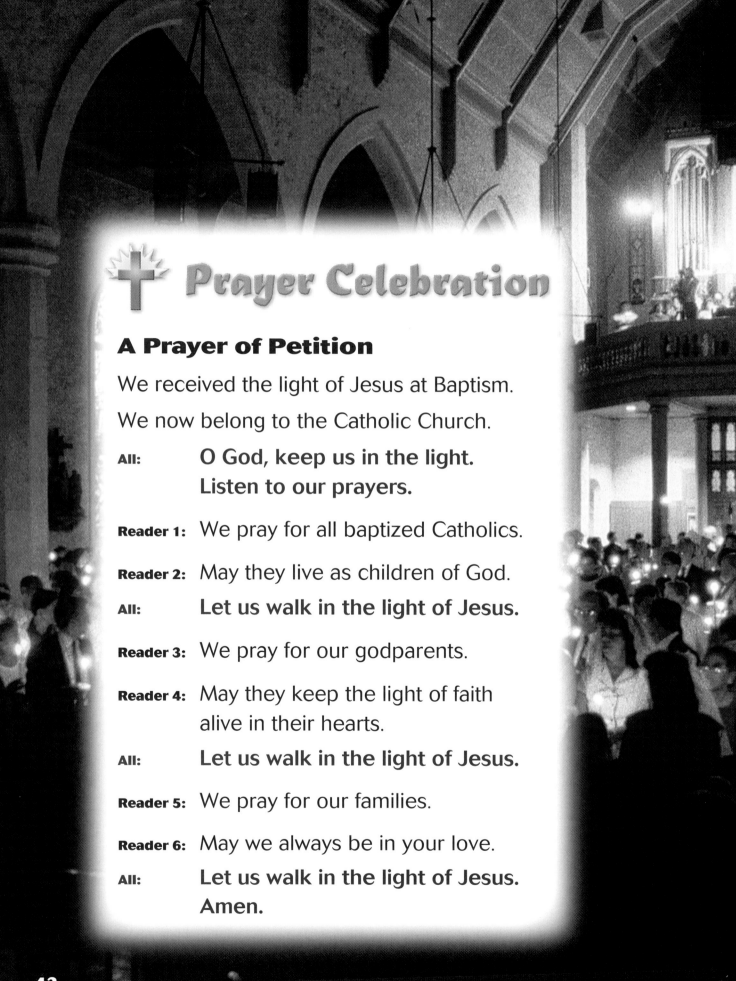

# ✝ Prayer Celebration

## A Prayer of Petition

We received the light of Jesus at Baptism.

We now belong to the Catholic Church.

**All:** **O God, keep us in the light.**
**Listen to our prayers.**

**Reader 1:** We pray for all baptized Catholics.

**Reader 2:** May they live as children of God.

**All:** **Let us walk in the light of Jesus.**

**Reader 3:** We pray for our godparents.

**Reader 4:** May they keep the light of faith
alive in their hearts.

**All:** **Let us walk in the light of Jesus.**

**Reader 5:** We pray for our families.

**Reader 6:** May we always be in your love.

**All:** **Let us walk in the light of Jesus.**
**Amen.**

**A** **Write** four signs for the Sacrament of Baptism.

_____     _____

_____     _____

_____     _____

_____     _____

**B** **Draw** a line to match the descriptions with the correct words.

1. A celebration of God's love and presence •     • Holy Spirit

2. The sin of the first man and woman •     • children of God

3. Who we receive at Baptism •     • sacrament

4. What we become at Baptism •     • original sin

# Faith in Action

**Godparents** At Baptism, godparents speak for the child being baptized. Godparents are special people. They help parents teach their child about the Catholic faith. Godparents show ways to love God. They are role models for their godchild.

## In Your Parish

**Activity** Maybe you have attended a baptism in your parish. What people in your family were there? What do you remember most about the celebration?

## In Everyday Life

**Activity** Write a thank you note to your own godparents.

# Take Home

FAMILY TIME

## Our Church Shows Us How to Live

Jesus shows us how to live in a way that pleases God. The saints have also shown us different ways to live a life that is godlike. The saints were men and women of various social and economic circumstances who lived extraordinary lives. They had this in common: They tried to live by the commandments, to love God, and to love their neighbors.

### ACTIVITY

**Name the Saints** Together, pick out an admirable quality or virtue possessed by each family member. Make a badge for each family "saint" with the person's name and saintly quality. Then wear your badges during a family meal.

## WEEKLY PLANNER

### On Sunday

Are there statues of saints in your church? Are any saints pictured in the stained-glass windows? Whose images do you see?

### On the Web

**www.blestarewe.com**

Visit our Web site for the saint of the day and the reflection question of the week.

### Saint of the Week

**Saint Peter Claver**
**(1581–1654)**

Peter Claver was a Jesuit missionary. He devoted his life and ministry to serving African slaves. He often lived in conditions almost as squalid as those of the people in his care.

**Patron Saint of:** interracial justice

**Feast Day:** September 9

### A Prayer for the Week

We thank you God, for giving us Saint Peter Claver who showed us how to live. Please give us the strength to live as he did. Amen.

# Take Home

FAMILY TIME

## ✝ Scripture Background

### In the Time of Jesus

**Samaritans** Samaritans lived in Israel around Mount Gerizin. Jews disliked Samaritans. Although sharing a common heritage with Jews, Samaritans had different religious customs. Jesus taught a parable involving a Samaritan who stopped to help when other fellow Jews did not. He also spoke of a Samaritan leper as the only grateful one of ten lepers cured. Jesus' message is that the Kingdom of God is for all people.

You can read about Samaritans in Luke 17:11–19, 10:29–35.

# OUR CATHOLIC TRADITION in Law

**Good Samaritan Law** The story of the Good Samaritan is famous. Many people know about the kind man who stopped to help the hurt stranger. The story is so famous that a good samaritan law has been enacted. This law requires people who have medical training to stop and help when they see an accident.

There was a time when those who had medical training wouldn't stop because they were afraid of being sued. This law protects the "Good Samaritans" from being sued, while requiring them to use their training to help the injured.

# 3 Our Church Shows Us How to Live

 **LET US PRAY** Love one another. Then everyone will know that you are my followers.

Based on John 13:35

## Share

Some people are heroes. They help others.
They show us how to live.

Find the heroes in these pictures.
Draw circles around them.

Who is your favorite real-life hero? Why?

Who are the Church's heroes?

# Hear & Believe

## ✝ Scripture  The Real Hero

One day, Jesus told a story about a hero.

A man was traveling by himself. Robbers attacked him. They beat him and took his money. He was left lying in the road, badly hurt.

Soon a religious leader came by. He saw the man, but he just kept going.

Next, a man who worked in the Temple came along. He also passed by without helping.

Then, a third man came by, riding a donkey. He was from the country of Samaria. He saw the hurt man on the road. He stopped at once. He washed the man's wounds. He put bandages on them. Then the man from Samaria put the hurt man on the donkey. He took him to an inn. There he paid the innkeeper to care for the man.

Based on Luke 10:29–35

48

# Heroes of Our Church

The Church has many heroes. Some are like the good man from Samaria. The Church has **saints** like Mary, the mother of Jesus. Saints are people who love God. They show great love for one another. Church heroes teach us how to act like Jesus.

## Our Church Teaches

All people are made to be **holy**. To be holy is to be like God. Through Baptism we are called to live good and holy lives.

How can we imitate Mary and all the saints?

**49**

# Respond

## Mary and Other Saints

Mary and other saints teach us how to live as Christians.

Mary is the greatest saint of all. She was a good mother to Jesus. She teaches us to trust God and to care for others.

Saint Peter Claver cared for people no one else cared about. He teaches us to reach out in love to everyone in need.

Saint Brigid sold what she had. She gave the money to people who were poor. She teaches us to share our blessings with others.

Saint Jerome loved to teach people how to read and understand the Bible. He teaches us to share the Word of God with others.

The Church has many heroes like these.
They all teach us how to love God and follow Jesus.

 Which saint is your favorite?
How can you follow this saint's example?

## Activity

Draw a picture of someone you know who is a hero. Or draw a picture of yourself acting in a good and holy way.

How can we ask holy people to pray for us?

 **Prayer Celebration**

## A Litany Prayer

A litany is a prayer that is said aloud.

A leader names saints or other holy people.

After each one, we ask the saint or persons to pray for us.

| Leader: | All: |
|---|---|
| Holy Mary, Mother of God, | pray for us. |
| Saint Peter Claver, | pray for us. |
| Saint Brigid, | pray for us. |
| Saint Jerome, | pray for us. |
| All who help the poor and the hungry, | pray for us. |
| All who care for the weak and the sick, | pray for us. |
| All holy men and women, | pray for us. |

**All:** **Heavenly God, may we follow the example of your saints and other holy people. May we always try to help people in need. Amen.**

# 3 Chapter Review

**A** **Circle** the words to complete the sentences.

1. People who show great love for others and for God are _____.
   old        saints        selfish

2. To be like God is to be _____.
   holy        pretty        rich

3. We become holy by loving _____ and other people.
   God        stories        things

4. Mary is the mother of _____.
   Brigid        Jerome        Jesus

**B** **Write** one way that you can be like Mary.

_____

_____

_____

_____

_____

# Faith in Action

**Helping Hands Ministry**  People in this ministry serve people who need help with tasks. Someone may need help to replace a ceiling light bulb, or recycle newspapers. Members may read letters to neighbors with poor vision. They reach out to anyone who needs a helping hand.

## In Your Parish

**Activity**  Name two ways that people in your parish treat others with kindness.

## In Everyday Life

**Activity**  What should you do? Place the number of the problem in front of the best answer.

**1** A group makes fun of a teacher.

**2** You see an older boy grab the lunch of a younger boy.

**3** You have a friend who is a bully.

_____ Ask yourself if you want that kind of friend.

_____ Report what you see to an adult.

_____ Do not laugh with them.

# Take Home

FAMILY TIME

# We Praise and Thank God

Saint Augustine said those who sing pray twice. He was telling us that raising our voices in song pleases God. This chapter presents the value of song as a form of prayer and the value of prayers of thanks and praise.

## ACTIVITY

**Name That Hymn** Play "Name That Hymn!" with your family. You can hum, play a musical instrument, or sing "la-la-la" to the tune of a favorite hymn. Let the others guess the title. Then invite them to sing along, if they know the words.

## WEEKLY PLANNER

### On Sunday

Even if you don't usually join in the singing at Mass, try it this week. Then, as Saint Augustine said, you will "pray twice."

### On the Web

**www.blestarewe.com**

 Visit our Web site for the saint of the day and the reflection question of the week.

### Saint of the Week

 **Pope Saint Gregory the Great (c. 540–604)**

As pope, Gregory the Great reformed the Church and gave generously to the poor. Pope Gregory I helped bring Christianity to England. He is credited with initiating Gregorian chant.

**Patron Saint of:** singers and musicians
**Feast Day:** September 3

### A Prayer for the Week

Thank you, Lord, for giving us life. May we use our voices to sing thanks and praise to you. Amen.

# Getting ready for Chapter 4
# Take Home

FAMILY TIME

## ✠ Scripture Background

### Before the Time of Jesus

**Psalms**   The Book of Psalms is an Old Testament collection of 150 songs, laments, and other types of prayers. Psalms have varied intentions: some glorify God, some offer praise and thanksgiving, some are wisdom psalms, others are petitions or laments, and still others are historical. David is considered to be the author of many psalms. Because psalms were also written after David's death, they can be considered a record of Israel's existence over time.

You can read Psalms 92 and 149 as examples of psalms of thanksgiving and praise.

## OUR CATHOLIC TRADITION in Music

**Gregorian Chant**   Since the seventh century the Church has been expressing its praise of God musically through Gregorian chant. Named after Pope Gregory I, chant is a solemn form of singing that creates a harmony between words and melody. Because in some pagan religions music was used to stir up people, Christians were encouraged to have a kind of music that was prayerful. Gregorian chant met that standard. There were other kinds of chants before Gregorian chant, but it was more beautiful and developed than some of the others.

In recent years a group of monks put out a recording called *Chant* that proved to be very popular. It revived interest in Gregorian chant.

# 4 We Praise and Thank God

 Sing to the LORD a new song.

Psalm 149:1

# Share

Celebrations are important times.
People come together to give thanks.
They say "thank you" for special people or gifts.

 On the Fourth of July, we give thanks for freedom.

 On birthdays we give thanks for life.

 On Thanksgiving we give thanks for all our blessings.

 On Valentine's Day we give thanks for friends.

**1.** Write the name of a celebration you enjoyed.

_____
- - - - - - - - - - - - - - - - - - - - - - - - - - - - - - - -
_____

**2.** Write why you gave thanks.

_____
- - - - - - - - - - - - - - - - - - - - - - - - - - - - - - - -
_____
_____
- - - - - - - - - - - - - - - - - - - - - - - - - - - - - - - -
_____

Why do God's People give thanks?

# Hear & Believe

## ✝ Scripture   King David Gives Thanks

King David loved God. He liked to lead the
Jewish people in prayer. David liked to play the harp,
dance, and sing. He sang about God's goodness.
He thanked God for giving the people many gifts.

One day Jewish leaders brought the ark that
held God's laws into David's city. David ordered
musicians to play on their harps, lyres, and cymbals.
Then David sang out,

"How good it is to give God thanks and glory!
I sing praise to your name, O God.
Every morning you are kind to me.
You are with me all day and all night.
Your goodness fills me with gladness.
I am happy because of the gifts you
give to me."

Based on 1 Chronicles 15 and Psalm 92:1–5

## We Give Praise and Thanks

King David wrote many song-prayers called **psalms**. Our parish community sings special songs at Mass. We give **praise** and thanks to God with holy music.

## Our Church Teaches

**Prayer** is talking to and listening to God. There are many kinds of prayer. Some prayers give thanks to God. Some prayers give praise for God's goodness. We can pray alone. We can pray with others. We can sing or play music as we pray.

## Faith Words

**praise**
Praise is a joyful type of prayer. It celebrates God's goodness.

**prayer**
Prayer is talking to and listening to God.

How can we praise and thank God?

# Respond

## Glory to God

In the first part of the Mass, we usually sing "Glory to God." This special song is called the Gloria. It is a prayer of praise and thanks. This is how it begins.

Glory to God in the highest,
and peace to his people on earth.

Lord God, heavenly King,
almighty God and Father,
we worship you, we give you thanks,
we praise you for your glory.

The Order of Mass

# Activities

**1.** Write your own prayer of praise.

O God, I praise you for being

_____

_____

_____

_____

_____

_____

**2.** Write your own prayer of thanks.

O God, I thank you for

_____

_____

_____

_____

_____

_____

You will use these prayers in the Prayer Celebration.

How can we praise and thank God with song?

# ✝ Prayer Celebration

## A Prayer of Praise and Thanks

As members of our parish community, we give praise and thanks to God. We can say and sing our prayers.

**Leader:** Heavenly God, we praise you. We give thanks to you in song.

**All (sing):** "Glory to God . . ."

**Leader:** Let us share our prayers of praise and thanks.

**All (sing):** "Glory to God . . ."

O God, I praise you for being

kind and forgiving.

O God, I thank you for

keeping grandpa

healthy.

**Leader:** Heavenly God, we give you thanks. We praise you in song.

**All (sing):** "Glory to God . . ."

**A** **Think about** the story "King David Gives Thanks." Draw a line under the words that name something King David liked to do.

mop the floor      lead people in prayer

sing and dance      run in races

write psalms      give thanks to God

**B** **Circle** the best answer.

1. What do we call an important time when people come together to give thanks?
   psalm    prayer    ark

2. What is a joyful type of prayer that celebrates God's goodness?
   praise    thanksgiving    sorrow

3. What is a prayer that shows gratitude for something God has done?
   praise    thanksgiving    joy

4. What do we call the prayers that King David wrote?
   psalms    impressions    creeds

# Faith in Action

**A Song Leader**   We can praise God in song. When we sing in church, we often have a music leader called a 'cantor.' A cantor loves to sing praises to God. The cantor leads us in singing holy songs.

**In Everyday Life**

**Activity**   Think about holy songs you like to sing. Who taught you these songs? Whom can you teach to sing?

**In Your Parish**

**Activity**   Circle the musical instruments used in your parish.

# We Ask God's Forgiveness

God is always ready to forgive us when we sin. God calls us to be sorry for the wrongs we have done. He wants us to forgive others who have wronged us.

*Rejoice with me because
I have found my lost sheep.*
Luke 15:6

God is like a shepherd who is happy to find his lost sheep. God rejoices when we are sorry for our sins.

# Psalm 51: Be Merciful, O Lord

*Psalm 51*

*Music by Marty Haugen*

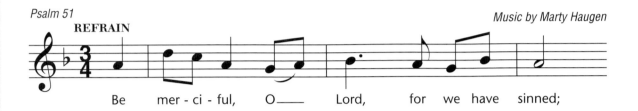

Be mer-ci-ful, O—— Lord, for we have sinned;

be—— mer-ci-ful, O—— Lord, for we have sinned.——————

**VERSE**

1. Have mercy on me, God, in your kindness,
   in your compassion, blot out my offense.
   O wash me more and more from my guilt and my sorrow,
   and cleanse me from all of my sin.
   *Refrain*

2. My offenses, truly I know them,
   and my sins are always before me;
   against you alone have I sinned, O Lord,
   what is evil in your sight I have done.
   *Refrain*

3. Create in me a clean heart, O God,
   put your steadfast spirit in my soul.
   Cast me not away from your presence, O Lord,
   and take not your spirit from me.
   *Refrain*

4. Give back to me the joy of your salvation,
   let your willing spirit bear me up
   and I shall teach your way to the ones who have wandered,
   and bring them all home to your side.
   *Refrain*

# Take Home

FAMILY TIME

# We Can Choose What is Good

Saint Thomas Aquinas, a Dominican priest and great theologian, proclaimed that humans always tended toward the good. But how do we figure out what the good is? It may feel good to finish the last of a box of candy, but others in our family might not see it as good. We try to form a good conscience to help us identify what is good and then try to conform our behavior to our conscience. Being Catholic helps us understand that God gives us free choice, and yet he is always ready to forgive us when we choose to sin.

## ACTIVITY

**Pick-up Sticks**  Did you ever play pick-up sticks? If so, you know that the sticks fall and you have to pick them up moving only the stick you are taking away. Play pick-up sticks with your child. Discuss how the game is like making moral choices. You need to choose carefully in order to succeed.

## WEEKLY PLANNER

### On Sunday

During the Penitential Rite, reflect on the choices you made during the week. Thank God for his guidance.

### On the Web

**www.blestarewe.com**

Visit our Web site for the saint of the day and the reflection question of the week.

### Saint of the Week

**Saint Peter of Saint Joseph Betancur**
**(1619–1667)**

Peter lived as a shepherd. He moved to the city to become a Third Order Franciscan. In 2002, San Pedro de San Jose Betancur became the first canonized native of Guatemala.

**Patron Saint of:** Guatemala
**Feast Day:** April 18

A Prayer for the Week

Lord, thank you for giving us the freedom to choose. Help us to use this gift to make right choices. Help us to be caring like Saint Peter of Saint Joseph Betancur. Amen.

# Take Home

FAMILY TIME

## ✚ Scripture Background

### In the Time of Jesus

**Inheritance**   Israelite tradition held that the eldest son would inherit the property and holdings of the father. The primary aim was to preserve the territory within each clan. Further biblical legislation also established the right of the firstborn to inherit twice as much as his brothers. In the Parable of the Forgiving Father, the younger son has already taken his share. So when the elder son is told that all that the father has is his, it literally means everything.

You can read this parable in Luke 15:11–32.

## OUR CATHOLIC TRADITION in Art

### Return of the Prodigal Son

The Rembrandt painting titled *Return of the Prodigal Son* depicts the story Jesus told of the young man who left his family and squandered his fortune. Thinking he would be better off as a servant on his father's farm than living as he was—poor, hungry, and alone—he returned home. As this painting shows, his father welcomed him back as a son, not as a servant.

Henri Nouwen based his book, *The Return of the Prodigal Son* on Rembrandt's painting.

# 5 We Can Choose What is Good

**LET US PRAY** Love the LORD, your God, and obey his word.

Based on Deuteronomy 30:20

# Share

We make many choices every day. Some choices are easy, but some are hard. Some are right, but others are wrong.

Draw a happy face for each good choice below.
Draw a sad face for each bad choice.

**1.** Tom does not share with his friends.

**2.** Juanita tells her dad the truth.

**3.** Wes obeys his mom and turns off the TV.

**4.** Mary takes a dollar that is not hers.

How do we know what is right and wrong?

# Hear & Believe

## ✝ Scripture The Forgiving Father

Once there was a man who had two sons. The younger son said, "I know you plan to give me money when I am older. May I have it now?" So his father gave him the money.

The boy moved far away. Soon, he had spent every cent! He was hungry and had no place to live.

The boy was sorry for the wrong choices he had made. He had wasted the money and hurt his father. The boy made up his mind to go home. He would ask his father to forgive him.

While the boy was still far from home, his father saw him. He ran to greet his son. "I'm sorry," the boy said, but his father had already forgiven him. The man hugged his son. Then he gave the boy a big "welcome home" party.

Based on Luke 15:11–24

# Knowing Right from Wrong

God lets us choose what to do. We call this **free choice**. The boy in the story knew he had done wrong. His **conscience** told him so. Our conscience tells us what is right or wrong.

## Our Church Teaches

We **sin** when we choose to do hurtful things on purpose. When we sin, we hurt our friendship with God and with other people. He wants us to be sorry for our sins. God loves us very much. When we do wrong, he is ready to show us mercy. God is ready to forgive us.

How can we practice making good choices?

# Respond

## Making Good Choices

Mrs. Rabbit said, "Peter, you and your sisters may play outdoors. But stay away from Mr. McGregor's garden!"

Peter's sisters obeyed their mother. Peter made a bad choice. He went into the garden and ate a lot of vegetables. Mr. McGregor saw Peter and began to chase him. Peter ran home as fast as he could.

Peter felt sick from eating so much. So Mrs. Rabbit gave him a warm drink. She put him to bed. He missed having a nice supper with his mom and his sisters.

**?** What bad choice did Peter make?

# Activity

We can practice making good choices every day. Unscramble the letters to complete the sentence for each picture.

**t h g i f**

Joey chooses not to

___ ___ ___ ___ ___
___ i ___ h ___ .

**r h a s e**

Tonya is happy to

___ ___ ___ ___ ___
___ h ___ r ___ .

**t r t u h**

Lily decides to tell the

___ ___ ___ ___ ___
t ___ ___ t ___ .

How can we celebrate the gift of free choice?

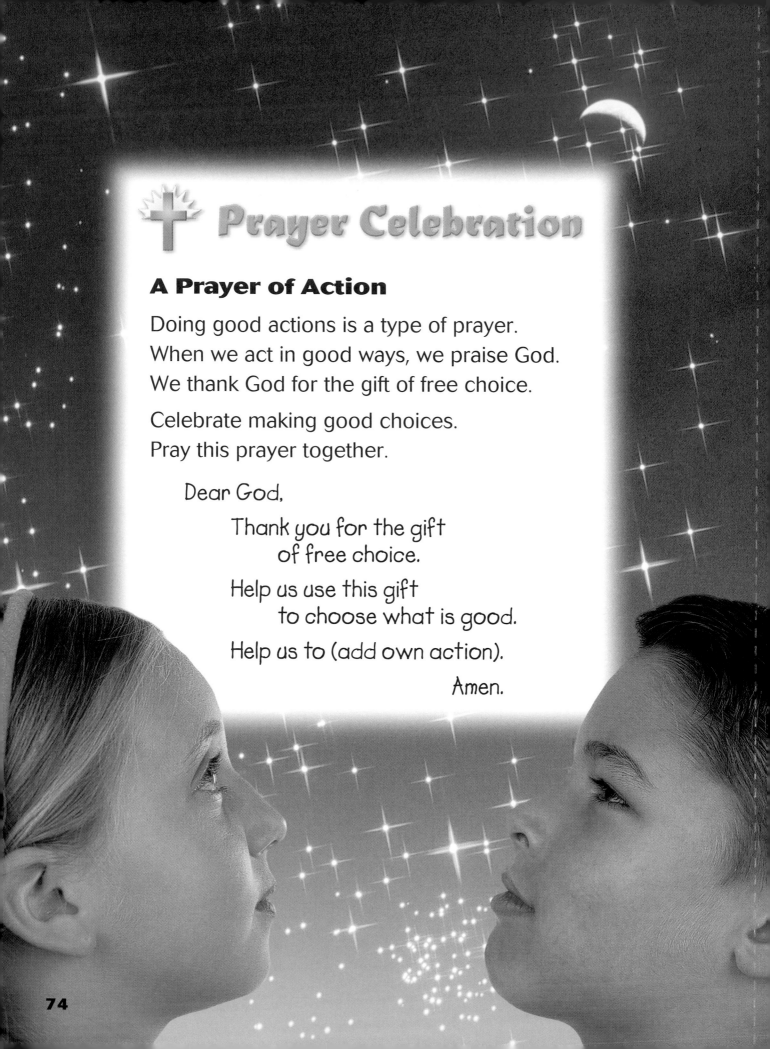

# ✟ Prayer Celebration

## A Prayer of Action

Doing good actions is a type of prayer.
When we act in good ways, we praise God.
We thank God for the gift of free choice.

Celebrate making good choices.
Pray this prayer together.

Dear God,

Thank you for the gift
of free choice.

Help us use this gift
to choose what is good.

Help us to (add own action).

Amen.

**A** **Circle** the words that best complete the sentences.

1. God gives us a _____ to help us know right from wrong.

   **conscience**   **free choice**   **sin**

2. When we do hurtful things on purpose, we _____.

   **forgive**   **love**   **sin**

3. God lets us choose what to do. We call this _____.

   **conscience**   **free choice**   **sin**

4. God wants us to be _____ for our sins.

   **angry**   **happy**   **sorry**

**B** **Draw a line** to connect the parts of each sentence.

1. The boy who left home knew   •          • the gift of free choice.

2. Before the boy said, "I'm sorry,"   •          • he had done wrong.

3. We thank God for   •          • his father had forgiven him.

# Faith in Action

**A Parish Council** Members of a parish council help the pastor. They help him make choices for the parish. They plan programs. They may decide ways to improve the church building. The pastor and the parish council try to make good choices.

## In Everyday Life

**Activity** Some families meet together to make choices. They listen to the needs of one another. Talk about ways family meetings can be helpful.

## In Your Parish

**Activity** One parish has chosen how to spend its money. Find their choices.

Help the Homeless

A Pony to Ride

Plant Trees

Drums for All

Food for Hungry

# Take Home

FAMILY TIME

# We Celebrate God's Forgiveness

One of the great joys of Christian life is that we can always trust in God's mercy. When we ask for God's mercy and are forgiven, we are reconciled to God. Even though we turn away from God when we sin, God never turns away from us. He is always ready to welcome us back.

## ACTIVITY

**Pretzels** Buy some frozen bread dough and thaw it. With your child, break off small pieces and roll them into ropes. Form a loop and then bring the ends of the loop up and cross them. Sprinkle salt on the pretzels and bake them. Share with your child that the pretzel shape represents an attitude of prayer, with arms crossed.

# WEEKLY PLANNER

## On Sunday

During the prayer before Communion, "Lord, I am not worthy...," remember that God is always ready to forgive.

## On the Web

**www.blestarewe.com**

 Visit our Web site for the saint of the day and the reflection question of the week.

## Saint of the Week

 **Saint Edith Stein** **(1891–1942)**

Edith Stein converted from Judaism to Catholicism and became a Carmelite nun. She was captured by the Nazis and taken to Auschwitz where she helped others until her death. She was canonized in 1998.

**Patron Saint of:** World Youth Day
**Feast Day:** August 9

 A Prayer for the Week

I'm sorry, Lord, for the things I have done to hurt others. Help me forgive others when they hurt me. Merciful God, I trust in your love and forgiveness. Amen.

# Take Home

FAMILY TIME

## ✝ Scripture Background

### In the Time of the Early Church

**Reconciliation** Reconciliation most often refers to the new relationship between God and humanity brought about by Christ's redemptive acts. Through Christ's death on the cross, humanity achieves peace with God. In many of Paul's letters, the idea of reconciliation goes beyond God and the individual to include the reconciliation of Jew and Gentile. Paul further describes a need for reconciliation of the world with God.

You can read a description of reconciliation in Romans 5:8–11.

## OUR CATHOLIC TRADITION in Interfaith Relations

**Jewish-Catholic Relations**
Pope John Paul II apologized to the Jewish people for the prejudice some Catholics have shown them throughout history. He asked the Jews for forgiveness. This was an important decision. The Pope was speaking as the head of the Catholic Church, in the name of all its members. In speaking to all of the Jewish people, he apologized for all the injustices inflicted upon the Jews by any Catholic people. It was an important move toward reconciliation between two peoples who worship the same God.

# 6 We Celebrate God's Forgiveness

 LORD, you are kind and forgiving.

Based on Psalm 86:5

# Share

Sometimes we say or do things that hurt other people. We can lose their friendship.

Put the pictures in order. In the boxes write 1, 2, 3, and 4. Then read the story about losing a friend and then making up.

Oops!

Hey! That's not fair!

Gina, let's race.

Sure, Dan!

I'm sorry. I won't do it again.

OK. Let's race again.

I won!

You cheated!

How can we make up with God?

# Hear & Believe

## Worship Making Up

The Sacrament of **Reconciliation**, or Penance, celebrates the gift of God's forgiveness. Follow Pat through her celebration of the sacrament.

**Welcome** Father Lee greets Pat. Together they make the Sign of the Cross.

**Reading** Father reads from the Bible. Pat hears about God's love and forgiveness.

**Confession** Pat talks about, or confesses, her sins. She knows Father Lee cannot tell anyone what she says in confession. He asks Pat to say a prayer or do a kind act. This will make up for what she has done wrong. This prayer or action is called a **penance**.

**Prayer of Sorrow** Pat says a prayer of sorrow, called the Act of Contrition. She tells God she is sorry. She will try not to sin again.

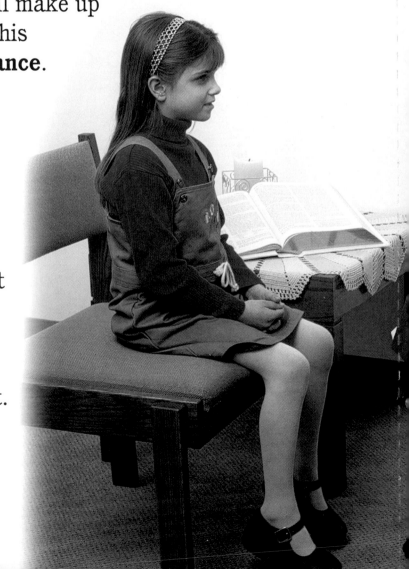

**Absolution** Father Lee asks God to forgive Pat. He gives Pat **absolution** in the name of the Father, Son, and Holy Spirit. Absolution is the forgiveness of God, given through the priest. Then Father Lee gives thanks and says, "Go in peace." Pat answers, "Amen."

## A Sacrament of Healing

When we have sinned, we need to say we are sorry. We need to ask for forgiveness. In Reconciliation, God heals us by forgiving our sins. God brings us peace.

## Our Church Teaches

The Sacrament of Reconciliation helps us make peace with God and the Catholic Church. The gift of God's **grace** helps us stay away from sin. Grace is God's loving presence in our lives.

GO TO page 15 to pray a prayer of sorrow.

**We Believe**

In the Sacrament of Reconciliation, we celebrate God's love, peace, and forgiveness.

**Faith Words**

**Reconciliation**
Reconciliation is a sacrament of healing that celebrates God's love and forgiveness.

**absolution**
Absolution is the forgiveness of God through the priest in the Sacrament of Reconciliation.

How can we practice being people who forgive?

# Respond

## Time to Forgive

Andy and Mark's father built them a treehouse. It was a great treehouse! Andy wanted to play in it with his friends. He did not want his little brother Mark with them.

One day, Mark just could not wait any longer for his turn. So he climbed up the ladder. "It's my turn now," he said.

Andy pushed him away. Mark fell off the ladder and broke his arm. He had to wear a cast for a long time. Andy felt sorry for what happened. He did not mean to hurt Mark.

**?** How could Andy make up with Mark?

# Activities

**1.** Complete the sentences with these forgiveness words.

sorry    forgive    make up

Andy and Mark should

_____

- - - - - - - - - - - - - - - - - - - - - - - - - - - - - -

_____.

Andy should say to Mark, "I am

_____

- - - - - - - - - - - - - - - - - - - - - - - - - - - - - -

_____."

Mark should say to Andy, "I

_____

- - - - - - - - - - - - - - - - - - - - - - - - - - - - - -

_____ you."

**2.** Write 1, 2, 3, and 4 to put the parts of the Sacrament of Reconciliation in order.

☐ pray a prayer of sorrow

☐ be given a penance

☐ receive absolution

☐ confess sins

**How can we celebrate God's forgiveness?**

# Prayer Celebration

## A Reconciliation Prayer

During Mass, we tell God we are sorry for our sins. We ask God to have mercy on us. We ask for forgiveness.

**Leader:** Lord Jesus, you help us live in peace with one another and with God the Father.

**All:** **Lord, have mercy.**

**Leader:** Lord Jesus, you heal the hurt that is caused by sin.

**All:** **Christ, have mercy.**

**Leader:** Lord Jesus, you pray to your Father for us.

**All:** **Lord, have mercy.**

**Leader:** May almighty God have mercy on us, forgive us our sins, and bring us to everlasting life.

**All:** **Amen.**

The Order of Mass

**A** **Complete** each sentence. Draw a line to the correct word.

1. In Reconciliation, we _____ our sins to a priest.

    ●     ● absolution

2. _____ is a sacrament of healing that celebrates God's love and forgiveness.

    ●     ● confess

3. The forgiveness of God in the name of the Father, Son, and Holy Spirit is _____.

    ●     ● grace

4. The loving presence of God in our lives is _____.

    ●     ● Reconciliation

**B** **Write** your own prayer asking forgiveness from God.

_____

- - - - - - - - - - - - - - - - - - - - -

_____

- - - - - - - - - - - - - - - - - - - - -

_____

- - - - - - - - - - - - - - - - - - - - -

_____

Amen.

# Faith in Action

**A Parish Priest**   A parish priest serves his parish in many ways. He reads the Word of God and preaches. A priest helps people when someone they love dies. He visits people in the hospital. Children enjoy stories the priest tells about Jesus.

**In Everyday Life**

**Activity**   When have you seen a priest from your parish at a place other than church?

**In Your Parish**

**Activity**   Draw a line from each activity to show when you think a priest would do it.

ride a bike

baptize a baby

say Mass

eat pizza

play baseball

hear confession

IN CHURCH

NOT IN CHURCH

# Take Home

FAMILY TIME

# We Think About Our Choices

This chapter deals with making choices and presents the Ten Commandments. The Commandments serve as a guide against which we measure our choices. Children learn that they are responsible for their actions. They learn that when they choose to do wrong, they sin. They also consider the differences among mistakes, venial sins, and mortal sins.

## ACTIVITY

**Choose a Game**  Play a board game as a family. Board games that involve choices help to illustrate the point of this chapter. Playing one of these games will demonstrate how the choices we make lead to consequences.

## WEEKLY PLANNER

### On Sunday

Talk with your family about ways to honor the Sabbath, such as going to Mass, avoiding conflict, and thinking about what God wants you to do.

### On the Web

**www.blestarewe.com**

Visit our Web site for the saint of the day and the reflection question of the week.

### Saint of The Week

**Saint Andrew the Apostle**

Andrew and his brother, Peter, fished for a living in the Sea of Galilee. A disciple of John the Baptist, Andrew was the first apostle called by Jesus. He then brought Peter to Jesus.

**Patron Saint of:** Russia and Scotland
**Feast Day:** November 30

A Prayer for the Week

Jesus, help us to follow the example of Andrew by placing our trust in you. Help us to take responsibility for our actions. Amen.

# Take Home

FAMILY TIME

## ✠ Scripture Background

### Before the Time of Jesus

**Mount Sinai**   Mount Sinai is part of the mountain range of Mount Horeb. It is sometimes called Mount Horeb. The Israelites believed that God dwelt on Sinai because Moses received the Ten Commandments from God there. During the Exodus from Egypt, the Israelites lived at the base of the mountain. In Galatians 4:21–27, Paul compares Mount Sinai to the Heavenly Jerusalem to show Jesus' fulfillment of the redemptive promise.

For an account of Moses' experience, you can read Exodus 20:1–17.

# OUR CATHOLIC TRADITION in Film

**The Spitfire Grill**   This 1996 film offers a moving story of forgiveness and reconciliation. A young woman, Percy Talbot, has no home to return to after serving prison time. The owner of *The Spitfire Grill* gives her housing in exchange for her services as a waitress. Percy touches the lives of many in the town. She forms a strong relationship with the owner and another woman. They share issues of sorrow, loss, and ultimately redemption.

# 7 We Think About Our Choices

**LET US PRAY**

Teach me, O LORD, your ways.
Guide me in goodness and truth.

Based on Psalm 25:4–5

## Share

As we grow up, we learn to be responsible for our actions. We are responsible when we do our work. We are responsible when we take good care of things.

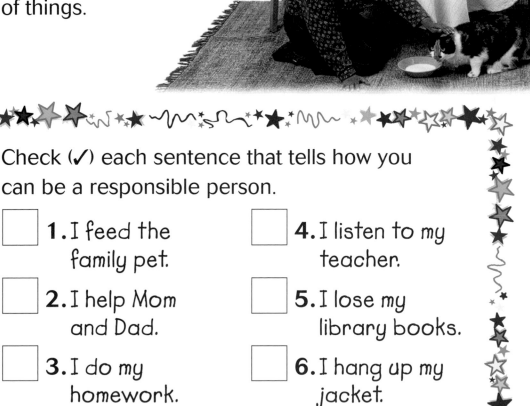

Check (✓) each sentence that tells how you can be a responsible person.

☐ **1.** I feed the family pet.

☐ **2.** I help Mom and Dad.

☐ **3.** I do my homework.

☐ **4.** I listen to my teacher.

☐ **5.** I lose my library books.

☐ **6.** I hang up my jacket.

How do we show we are responsible church members?

Name other ways to show that you are responsible.

# Hear & Believe

## ✝ Scripture  Moses on the Mountain

Moses was on a mountaintop when God spoke to him. God wanted to help everyone lead good lives. He gave Moses the laws called the **Ten Commandments**. These laws call for people to love and respect God and others. After receiving the laws, Moses went down the mountain. He told the Jewish people about these laws of God.

The Ten Commandments remind people to rest and pray on the Lord's day. They tell people to obey their parents, and to avoid telling lies or stealing. The commandments also say not to hurt other people nor be jealous of them.

Based on Exodus 20:1–17

# The Ten Commandments

The Ten Commandments are God's laws. God gave his people the Commandments to help them make good choices. Jesus learned these laws. He taught them to his followers. They help people know right from wrong.

## Our Church Teaches

When we know that something is wrong, and we do it anyway, we sin. Sin turns us away from God and other people. **Mortal sins** are serious sins. They separate us from our friendship with God. **Venial sins** are less serious sins. They weaken our friendship with God, but do not take it away.

## We Believe

God gave us the Ten Commandments to help us know how to lead good lives.

## Faith Words

**mortal sins**
Mortal sins are serious sins. They separate us from our friendship with God.

**venial sins**
Venial sins are less serious sins. They weaken our friendship with God.

How can we think about the Ten commandments?

# Respond

## An Examination of Conscience

We prepare to celebrate the Sacrament of Reconciliation. We think about the Ten Commandments. We think about how well we have followed each one. This is called an examination of conscience.

| God's Laws | My Actions |
| --- | --- |
| 1. Believe that there is only one God. | Do I believe in God and love God with all my heart? |
| 2. Respect the name of God. | Do I use the names of God, Jesus, Mary, and the saints with respect? |
| 3. Go to Mass on Sunday. | Do I celebrate Mass on Sunday? |
| 4. Respect your father and mother. | Do I respect and obey my parents? |
| 5. Take care of all that God has made. | Do I treat all God's creatures with respect? |
| 6. Treat your body as a gift from God. | Do I take good care of my body and respect the bodies of others? |
| 7. Respect the property of others. | Have I taken something that belongs to someone else? |
| 8. Always tell the truth. | Do I sometimes lie? |
| 9. Respect the families of others. | Do I treat other families with respect? |
| 10. Be content with what you have. | Am I ever jealous or greedy? |

Mistakes and sins are not the same. You might break a glass by mistake. You sin when you choose to do something you know is wrong.

## Activity

Follow the stone path. If the stone tells about a mistake, color the stone yellow. If it tells about a sin, color the stone red.

1. Oops! I spilled gravy on my new sweater.

2. I stole my brother's favorite cap.

3. I had a big fight with a friend.

4. I left the window open, and the rain came in.

5. I was jealous of my friend's new bike.

6. I lied about what happened to my homework.

7. I lost my lunch money.

8. I forgot to wish my cousin a happy birthday.

How can we celebrate thinking about our choices?

# ✝ Prayer Celebration

## A Thinking Prayer

**Leader:** Thinking is a special gift God has given us. We use this gift when making choices. We use it in prayer to ask God to forgive our sins.
Let us pray.

**Side 1:** God, our Father, sometimes we have not behaved.

**All:** **Forgive us and show us your mercy.**

**Side 2:** Sometimes we have fought.

**All:** **Forgive us and show us your mercy.**

**Side 1:** Sometimes we have been lazy.

**All:** **Forgive us and show us your mercy.**

**Side 2:** Sometimes we have told lies.

**All:** **Forgive us and show us your mercy. Amen.**

Based on the Rite of Penance

# 7 Chapter Review

**A** **Circle** the words that best complete the sentences.

1. Telling a lie is _____.
   **responsible**     **not responsible**     **okay**

2. God gave Moses laws called the _____ Commandments.
   **Great**          **Five**               **Ten**

3. The third commandment tells us to go to _____
   on Sunday.
   **Mass**           **meetings**           **movies**

4. The fifth commandment tells us to _____ all God made.
   **disrespect**     **take care of**       **use up**

5. Mistakes are never _____.
   **accidents**      **laws**               **sins**

**B** **Complete** the definitions.

1. Mortal sins are serious sins. They

   _____

   - - - - - - - - - - - - - - - - - - - - - - - - - - - - - -

   _____

   us from our friendship with God.

2. Venial sins are less serious sins. They

   _____

   - - - - - - - - - - - - - - - - - - - - - - - - - - - - - -

   _____

   our friendship with God.

# Faith in Action

**Community Outreach**   There are many ways for people to serve their parish. Some people belong to a community outreach ministry. They help workers find jobs. They write letters to public officials about the rights people have.

**In Your Parish**

**Activity**   Think about ways you help others in your parish. When have you treated someone fairly? How have you been kind to others?

**In Everyday Life**

**Activity**   In the first column are duties we have. In the second column are rights to match them. Draw a line to match each right with the responsibility that fits it.

| Duties | Rights |
|--------|--------|
| 1. Carol studies her lessons.  • | • FOOD |
| 2. Ben does not waste food at lunch.  • | • FAMILY |
| 3. Miguel goes to church with his family.  • | • SCHOOL |
| 4. Ann helps take care of her home.  • | • SHELTER |
| 5. Sandra respects her parents.  • | • RELIGION |

# Take Home

FAMILY TIME

# We Say We Are Sorry

When we choose to do wrong, we need to say we are sorry, to God and to any person we have hurt. The focus of this chapter is to learn to use prayer to tell God that we are sorry. When we do this, we admit that we have done wrong and recognize that we need to acknowledge it. Children will learn that prayer brings us closer to God and that, with the Holy Spirit's help, we can change.

## ACTIVITY

**How Many Ways?** With your child, think of several ways to say or show that you are sorry. Some examples are "Please forgive me," "I didn't mean to hurt you," giving a hug, and shaking hands. You might want to make a list of all the expressions and actions you have identified.

## WEEKLY PLANNER

### On Sunday

During the Sunday liturgy, ask God's forgiveness for wrong choices you made last week.

### On the Web

**www.blestarewe.com**

 Visit our Web site for the saint of the day and the reflection question of the week.

### Saint of The Week

 **Saints Elizabeth and Zachary (first century)**

Elizabeth was Mary's cousin. She and Zachary were the parents of John the Baptist. The angel Gabriel told Zachary their son would be filled with the Holy Spirit. John's parents trusted God.

**Patron Saints of:** pregnant women

**Feast Day:** November 5

 A Prayer for the Week

O Lord, may our family be as close as that of Elizabeth and Zachary. Help us to recognize wrongs we have done to family members. Strengthen us to admit our faults and say we are sorry. Amen.

# Take Home

## ✚ Scripture Background

### In the Time of Jesus

**Repentance** Early Jews expressed collective, rather than personal, guilt. Group liturgies were common, stressing fasting and the confession of sin. Later, prophets began calling people to individual responsibility to bring about justice, kindness, and humility. Both John the Baptist and Jesus called for repentance connected to the coming of the Kingdom. They called on people to express sorrow and to turn away from sin.

You can read of John's call to repentance in Matthew 3:1–17.

# OUR CATHOLIC TRADITION in Music

**Fiddler on the Roof** *Fiddler on the Roof* was a Broadway musical and a movie. It tells the story of a Russian Jewish family before the Russian Revolution. One of the most poignant songs, "Sunrise, Sunset," sung by the mother and father, is about how quickly time passes in a family and how quickly children grow up. This song echoes the sentiment of Catholic parents as well. How do children grow up so fast? This timely song reminds us that we should nurture our relationship with our children, because they won't be with us forever.

# 8 We Say We Are Sorry

When a sinner is sorry, there is great joy in heaven.

Based on Luke 15:7

# Share

There are many ways to say "I'm sorry."
You can say it with words like "Let's make up."
You can say it with an action like a hug.
Tell another good way to say "I'm sorry."

Make a card to tell someone you are sorry for something. Print what you want to say.

_____

Dear _____,
_____
_____
_____
_____
_____

Love,
_____
_____

How can we tell God we are sorry?

# Hear & Believe

## ✝ Scripture  Return to God!

John the Baptist was a holy man. He told other people how to find God's forgiveness.

**John:** Return to God! Repent. God's Kingdom is coming!

**Woman:** What does repent mean?

**John:** Repent means to be truly sorry for your sins.

**Boy:** What else does repent mean?

**John:** It means that you really want to change.

**Girl:** Is that all we need to do to return to God?

**John:** No. You must also do **penance**. Penance is a prayer or an act to make up for the harm caused by sin.

Many people heard John's words. They confessed their sins. They told God they were sorry. Then John baptized them in the river.

Based on Matthew 3:1–8

## Returning to God

Sin separates us from God. John the Baptist wanted people to go back to God. We can return to God by telling him we are sorry for our sins. When we are sorry for our sins, we feel **contrition**. Contrition means to be sorry and to want to do better.

### Our Church Teaches

To show that we are sorry for our sins, we pray an **act of contrition**. This is a prayer of sorrow. In this prayer we promise to try not to sin again. When we are sorry for our sins, the Holy Spirit helps us do better.

### Faith Words

**contrition**
Contrition means to be sorry and to want to stay away from sin.

**act of contrition**
An act of contrition is a prayer that tells God we are sorry for our sins.

How can we show we are sorry for sin?

# Respond

## A Penance Service

Matt and Susan went to a penance service. Many other people were there, too. Everyone had come to show that they wanted to return to God. They listened to a story that Jesus once told. It is about a shepherd and a lost sheep.

God is like the shepherd who had one hundred sheep. One sheep got lost. The shepherd went to look for it. When he found the sheep, the shepherd was very happy. In the same way, there is great joy in heaven when a sinner repents.

Based on Luke 15:4–7

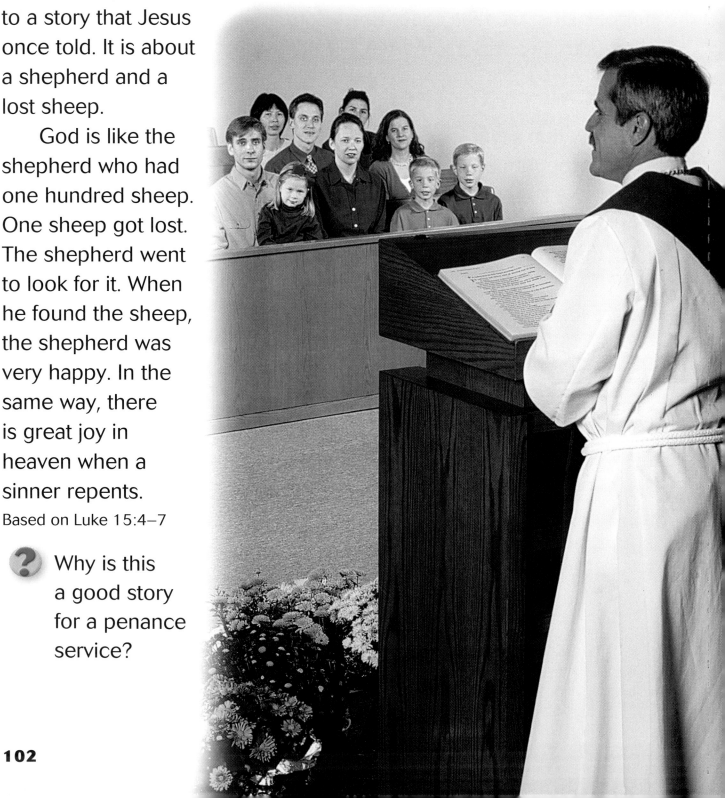

 Why is this a good story for a penance service?

# Activity

Use the secret code to write the missing letters.
Then read the prayer of sorrow.

**Secret Code**

| 1 | 2 | 3 | 4 | 5 | 6 | 7 | 8 | 9 | 10 | 11 | 12 | 13 |
|---|---|---|---|---|---|---|---|---|----|----|----|----|
| A | B | C | D | E | F | G | H | I | J  | K  | L  | M  |

| 14 | 15 | 16 | 17 | 18 | 19 | 20 | 21 | 22 | 23 | 24 | 25 | 26 |
|----|----|----|----|----|----|----|----|----|----|----|----|----|
| N  | O  | P  | Q  | R  | S  | T  | U  | V  | W  | X  | Y  | Z  |

___ ___ ___ ___ ___ ___, ___
6   1   20   8   5   18   9

___ ___ ___ ___ ___ ___ ___
1   13   19   15   18   18   25

___ ___ ___ ___ ___ ___
6   15   18   1   12   12

___ ___ ___ ___ ___ ___.
13   25   19   9   14   19

How can
we return
to God?

103

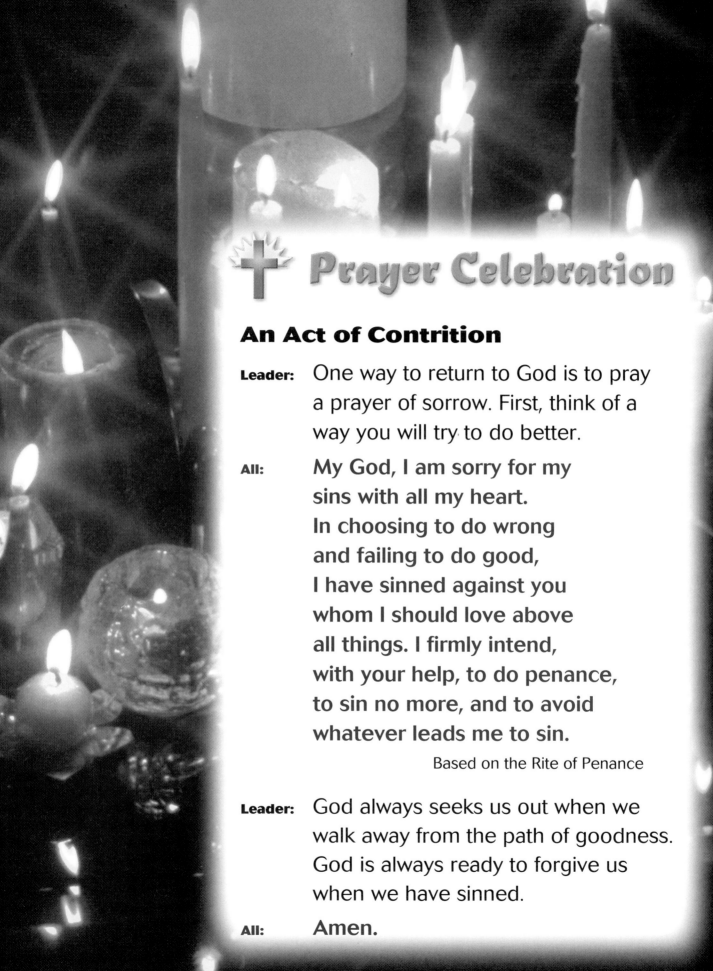

# ✝ Prayer Celebration

## An Act of Contrition

**Leader:** One way to return to God is to pray a prayer of sorrow. First, think of a way you will try to do better.

**All:** My God, I am sorry for my
sins with all my heart.
In choosing to do wrong
and failing to do good,
I have sinned against you
whom I should love above
all things. I firmly intend,
with your help, to do penance,
to sin no more, and to avoid
whatever leads me to sin.

Based on the Rite of Penance

**Leader:** God always seeks us out when we walk away from the path of goodness. God is always ready to forgive us when we have sinned.

**All:** Amen.

**A** **Complete** each sentence by drawing a line to the correct word.

1. _____ means to be sorry and to want to do better. •

• **act of contrition**

2. A prayer or act to make up for the harm caused by sin is called a _____. •

• **contrition**

3. To show that we are sorry, we pray an _____. •

• **penance**

**B** **Draw or write.** What did Jesus say happens in heaven when a sinner repents?

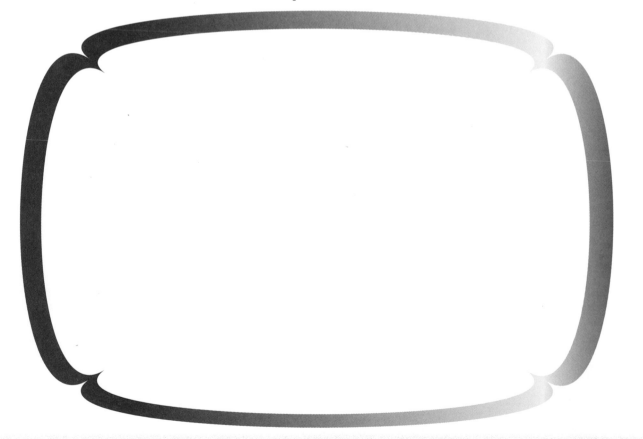

# Faith in Action

**A Sacristan**   Before each Mass, a sacristan gets everything ready for the priest. The sacristan lights the candles on the altar and places the chalice nearby. Mass readings are opened to the right page. This minister helps the Mass go smoothly. This is a quiet but important ministry.

**In Your Parish**

**Activity**   Get this altar ready for Mass. Draw lines to put items in the right places.

**In Everyday Life**

**Activity**   Every job is important. Think of a time that you forgot to do your job. How did that affect others? How could you show you are sorry for this?

# We Celebrate the Word of God

The Word of God is Jesus Christ among us. When we listen to the Scripture readings, we are taught the way of the Gospel. We are inspired to live as true followers of Jesus.

> *But some seed fell on rich soil, and produced fruit, a hundred or sixty or thirtyfold. Whoever has ears ought to hear.*
>
> Matthew 13:8–9

The farmer plants seeds that will grow into food. Like seeds, our faith grows when we listen to God's Word.

# Go and Listen

*Words and Music by Robert J. Batastini*

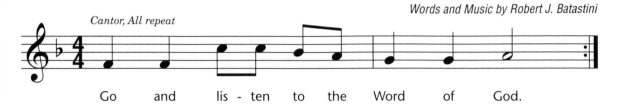

Go and lis - ten to the Word of God.

God has the words of ev - er - last - ing life.

# Take Home

FAMILY TIME

# We Learn About God's Love

The Bible is a book filled with many kinds of literature, such as stories, letters, prayers, and songs. The Bible tells of God's love for us, from the moment of creation on. This chapter encourages children to be aware of the Bible as a tool for learning about God's gift of creation, his love for us, and his gift of his Son, Jesus.

## ACTIVITY

**Creating with Clay** God made us out of clay, according to one account in Genesis. Together, take some clay and make something that shows your thanks to God for creating each family member and continuing to love you all your lives.

## WEEKLY PLANNER

### On Sunday

Listen to the readings at Mass. Then, later in the day, choose one of the readings to discuss with your family.

### On the Web

**www.blestarewe.com**

 Visit our Web site for the saint of the day and the reflection question of the week.

### Saint of the Week

 **Saint Angela Merici (1474–1540)**

Angela Merici wanted children and their families to learn to love God. She and her friends started teaching religion classes. They opened a school under the protection of St. Ursula.

**Patron Saint of:** the sick and people with disabilities
**Feast Day:** January 27

 **A Prayer for the Week**

Saint Angela Merici wanted to share the Word of God with others. O Lord, help us to open our hearts to your words in the Bible. Teach us to protect all that you have made. Amen.

# Take Home

## ✝ Scripture Background

### In the Time of Jesus

**Birds**   Because of its varied climates and types of environments, the Holy Land attracts many species of birds. The Bible refers to fifty different species. Over forty books in the Bible mention birds, such as eagles, owls, storks, quails, hens, and sparrows. In Jesus' time, all small birds were called sparrows. Jesus spoke of his Father's concern for all of creation, even small birds. Both Matthew and Luke refer to sparrows in their gospels.

You can read about attention given to sparrows in Matthew 10:27–33.

# OUR CATHOLIC TRADITION in Art

**Illumination**   The painstaking work of monks and artists of the Middle Ages has left us with some priceless treasures of Scriptures copied and illuminated by hand. *Illumination* is a kind of decoration that was often used to illustrate and highlight the first letter of a passage. Artists used bright colors and gold to intertwine pictures of flowers and animals in the letter, making it so fancy that it was sometimes difficult to figure out what letter it was supposed to be. But the artworks are extraordinarily detailed and beautiful. They show the reverence in which the artists held the Holy Scriptures.

# 9 We Learn About God's Love

**LET US PRAY** The LORD God took Adam and settled him in the garden of Eden to care for it.

Based on Genesis 2:15

## Share

The world that God created has mountains, forests, and deserts. It has rivers, lakes, and oceans.

The earth has many kinds of plants and animals, too. Name some plants and animals you know about.

Draw a picture of yourself taking care of something God created.

What does creation tell us about God?

# Hear & Believe

## ✝ Scripture  God Loves All Creation

One day, Jesus told his followers this story about God's love.

"Some people worry about what they will eat and drink. Other people worry about what clothes to wear. But I say, do not worry. Instead, look at the birds in the sky. God takes good care of them. Look at the flowers in the field. God takes good care of them, too.

"So have faith. God loves you even more than the birds and flowers. He is a loving Father who knows what you need. God will always take care of you."

Based on Matthew 6:25–34

## Ways We Learn About God

God is the creator of all things. In the **Bible** we read that he made all things good. God promises to take care of us. And, God asks us to take care of creation. The story Jesus told about taking care of creation is a Bible story. We read the **Word of God** in the Bible.

### Our Church Teaches

The Bible is also called **Scripture**. Scripture means "holy writings." All the teachings of Jesus are in the Bible. Jesus is the **Son of God**.

**GO TO** ▶ pages 17–21 to learn more about the Bible.

### We Believe

We learn about God's love for us from the Bible. He made all creation good. We are to care for God's creation.

### Faith Words

**Bible**
The Bible is the written Word of God.

**Son of God**
Son of God is a special title for Jesus. Jesus is God's only Son.

How can people show love for God's creation?

# Respond

## Caring for God's Creation

Where there had once been an empty lot there is now a community garden. Pat's family and other neighbors cleaned up the lot. They broke up the hard soil. Now they grow flowers, fruits, and vegetables there. They even recycle things to use in their garden. These neighbors are showing respect for the earth.

**?** How can you care for God's creation?

# Activities

1. Learn to sign the words "God cares for you."

 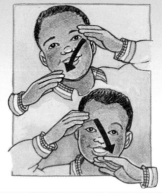 

| God | cares for | you. |

2. See the word CREATION below. Think of something God made that begins with each letter. Write the words on the lines. The first one is done for you.

C louds

R

E

A

T

I

O

N

How can the Bible help us celebrate God's love?

# Prayer Celebration

## A Psalm about Creation

**Leader:** We celebrate God's gift of creation with this Bible prayer. For each response, lift your arms high with your palms facing up.

**Reader 1:** You made the clouds and wind.

**Side 1:** **O God, you are great indeed!**

**Reader 2:** You made the land and seas.

**Side 2:** **O God, your works are wonderful!**

**Reader 3:** You made the sun and moon.

**Side 1:** **O God, you are great indeed!**

**Reader 4:** You made lakes and mountains.

**Side 2:** **O God, your works are wonderful!**

**Reader 5:** You made trees and birds.

**Side 1:** **O God, you are great indeed!**

**Leader:** How can we celebrate God's love?

**All:** **We will sing praise to God.**

Based on Psalm 104

**A** **List** five things that the Bible tells us God created.

_____

- - - - - - - - - - - - - - - - - - - - - - - - -

_____

_____

- - - - - - - - - - - - - - - - - - - - - - - - -

_____

_____

- - - - - - - - - - - - - - - - - - - - - - - - -

_____

**B** **Write** the letter for the missing word in each sentence.

| **A** Bible | **B** care | **C** creation | **D** Son | **E** worry |
| --- | --- | --- | --- | --- |

1. We learn about God's love for us from the ☐.

2. God takes care of all ☐.

3. Jesus tells us not to ☐.

4. Jesus is the ☐ of God.

5. God will always take ☐ of us.

# Faith in Action

**Green Thumbs Committee**  Senior citizens and young people work together on this committee. The older people are good at growing plants and trees. But, gardening is hard work. The young people help them. Together they show God respect for creation.

## In Your Parish

**Activity**  Think about ways your parish uses the gift of water. How does it use the gift of fire?

## In Everyday Life

**Activity**  Put a ✔ for things you already do for the Earth.
Put an ✘ for things you should not do.
Put a • for things you will do.

| Actions | Do Now | Not Do | Will Do |
|---|---|---|---|
| Recycle paper and plastic. | | | |
| Throw empty cans on the grass. | | | |
| Plant vegetables and flowers. | | | |
| Leave trash on the floor. | | | |
| Take care of pets. | | | |

FAMILY TIME

# We Listen to God's Word

In this chapter, children will come to realize that when we hear the Scripture readings, we are listening to God's Word. The children will learn the responses said during the Liturgy of the Word. They will also learn that the Nicene Creed is a prayer that states the beliefs that Catholics hold.

## ACTIVITY

**Good News** Put a "Remember the Good News" sign on your refrigerator. Share some good news with each other this week. This will prepare your child to learn about the "Good News" of the gospels.

Remember the Good News!

# WEEKLY PLANNER

## On Sunday
Show your child the Old and New Testaments in the Bible. Point out that the New Testament contains the gospel stories that tell about Jesus.

## On the Web
**www.blestarewe.com**
 Visit our Web site for the saint of the day and the reflection question of the week.

## Saint of the Week
**Saint Hilary of Poitiers (315–368)**

Hilary of Poiters was married and a father before he began to believe in God. As a result of reading the New Testament, he converted to Christianity. He was later named a bishop.

**Patron Saint of:** children with disabilities
**Feast Day:** January 13

A Prayer for the Week

Lord, we lift up our hearts, our minds, and our ears to your Word. Help us understand your Scriptures. Give us the gift of understanding, Lord. Amen.

# Take Home

FAMILY TIME

## ✝ Scripture Background

### In the Time of Jesus

**Crops**   The most important crops in the Holy Land were barley and wheat, since they formed the basis for bread and were food for animals. Usually, seed was sown after the autumn rains. Following winter rains and those of March and April, the barley was ready to be harvested. Wheat was harvested during the summer. After the sheaves were laid out, animals walked on them, cutting apart the stalks, the chaff, and the grain.

Read about the parable of the sower in Matthew 13:1–9, 18–23.

# OUR CATHOLIC TRADITION   in Church Design

**Pulpits**   Catholic churches usually have a crucifix, statues, a baptismal font, an altar, and a lectern. The lectern reminds us that God speaks to us. A lectern may also be called an ambo. Starting around the ninth century, churches had two stands, called ambos. One was for gospel readings and one was for readings from the letters. The one for the gospel became more and more ornate until, by the thirteenth century, it became known as the pulpit. The word *pulpit* comes from the Latin *pulpitum*, meaning "stage." These ornate pulpits were at first built in Italian churches. Over time, they have been made in many styles and materials, such as stone and iron.

# 10 We Listen to God's Word

Listening to God's Word is like building a house on rock.
A house like that will not fall down.

Based on Matthew 7:24–25

# Share

Most people like hearing a good story. The story can be funny, sad, or even scary. To enjoy a story, we need to be good listeners.

**1.** Who is the best storyteller you know?

_____

- - - - - - - - - - - - - - - - - - - - - - - - - - - - - - -

_____

**2.** What story do you like to listen to again and again?

_____

- - - - - - - - - - - - - - - - - - - - - - - - - - - - - - -

_____

**3.** Why do you like this story?

_____

- - - - - - - - - - - - - - - - - - - - - - - - - - - -

_____

_____

- - - - - - - - - - - - - - - - - - - - - - - - - - - -

_____

When do church members listen to the stories of Jesus?

# Hear & Believe

## Worship A Story About Listening

One day, Jesus told this story about listening to the Word of God.

"A farmer scattered seeds in his field. Some seeds fell on a path. Birds ate them up. Some fell on rocks. They dried up and died. Some seeds fell among thorns. The thorns grew and choked the seeds. Other seeds fell on good soil. They took root, grew, and produced good fruit.

"People are like the places where the farmer's seeds fell. People who do not try to understand God's Word are like the path. Some hear God's Word but remember it only a short time. They are like the rocks. Some people hear God's Word in church. But, they forget about it the rest of the week. They are like the soil with thorns. Other people hear God's Word and really listen to it. They are like the good soil. Faith grows in them."

Based on Matthew 13:1–9, 18–23

# Listening to God's Word

This Bible story tells what happens when we really listen to God's Word. Our faith grows. At Mass we listen to God's Word from the Bible.

## Our Church Teaches

During the **Liturgy of the Word** on Sunday, we listen to three Bible readings. The first one is from the Old Testament. The second and third readings are from the New Testament. The third reading is the **Gospel**. It tells the story of Jesus' life. After the Gospel, the priest or deacon gives a talk called a homily. The **homily** helps us understand the Bible readings we just heard. Then we all say the **Nicene Creed**. This prayer says what Catholics believe.

**GO TO** page 12 to pray the Nicene Creed and pages 17–21 to learn more about the Bible.

## We Believe

At Mass we listen to God's Word. The Nicene Creed tells about God's love for us. It tells what we believe.

## Faith Words

**Nicene Creed** Catholics tell what they believe when they pray the Nicene Creed at Mass.

How can we show we are listening during the Liturgy of the Word?

# Respond

## We Take Part at Mass

On Sundays, Juan takes part at Mass with the parish community. He joins others in singing. Juan likes hearing Bible stories about God and Jesus. He knows the responses to the Bible readings.

After the first and second Bible readings, the reader says, "The Word of the Lord."

Juan and others answer, "Thanks be to God."

Everyone stands for the Gospel. After the reading, the priest or deacon says, "The Gospel of the Lord."

Juan knows to answer, "Praise to you, Lord Jesus Christ."

Then Juan sits quietly and listens to the homily. He wants to learn how to be like Jesus.

# Activity

What word is missing in each sentence?

1. The first part of Mass is the Liturgy of the _____.

2. After the first reading we say, "_____ be to God."

3. The _____ tells the Good News about Jesus' life and teachings.

4. After the Gospel we say, "_____ to you, Lord Jesus Christ."

5. The talk given by the priest or deacon is called the _____.

6. The Nicene _____ is a prayer about what we believe as Catholics.

Now do the puzzle. Find and circle the missing words.

| A | C | B | E | C | F | H | G |
|---|---|---|---|---|---|---|---|
| I | W | J | K | R | L | T | M |
| G | O | S | P | E | L | H | N |
| O | R | P | Q | E | R | A | S |
| U | D | T | V | D | X | N | Y |
| H | O | M | I | L | Y | K | Z |
| B | A | P | R | A | I | S | E |

How can we celebrate with a prayer song?

# ✝ Prayer Celebration

## A Responsorial Psalm

**Leader:** After the first reading at Mass, we respond with a special prayer-song. This responsorial psalm is part of the Liturgy of the Word. Let us pray this psalm about creation together.

**Reader 1:** The seed that falls on good ground will yield a fruitful harvest.

**All:** **The seed that falls on good ground will yield a fruitful harvest.**

**Reader 2:** Our God, you take care of the earth and send rain to help the soil grow all kinds of crops.

**All:** **The seed that falls on good ground will yield a fruitful harvest.**

**Reader 3:** Your rivers never run dry, and you prepare the earth to produce much grain.

**All:** **The seed that falls on good ground will yield a fruitful harvest.**

Based on Lectionary for Masses with Children

# 10 Chapter Review

**A** **Draw a line** to connect the parts of each sentence.

1. People who listen to God's Word are like seeds that fall on _____.

   ●     ● good soil

2. At Mass we come together to listen to God's Word from the _____.

   ●     ● Nicene Creed

3. We call this part of Mass the Liturgy of the _____.

   ●     ● Word

4. Our _____ grows when we really listen to God's Word.

   ●     ● Bible

5. We state what we believe in a prayer called the _____.

   ●     ● faith

**B** **Number** the parts of the Liturgy of the Word in order.

_____ The priest explains the Gospel reading.

_____ We listen to a reading from the Old Testament.

_____ We pray the Nicene Creed.

_____ We listen to the Gospel.

_____ We sing a prayer-song.

# Faith in Action

**Lectors** People who read Scripture to the community at Mass are called lectors. They practice reading God's Word out loud before Mass. They read carefully so everyone can understand the Scripture stories.

## In Everyday Life

**Activity** Think about the difference between reading a story and hearing one. Read a Bible story. Then, listen to someone read it out loud. Which do you like best? Why?

## In Your Parish

**Activity** Draw yourself reading Scripture out loud in church.

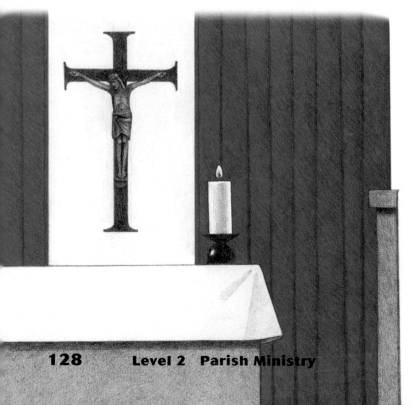

# Take Home

# We Act on God's Word

Jesus made the treatment of other human beings the focus of his time on earth. How we should think about and respond to others was the topic of many of Jesus' teachings. He gave us many examples of service. Children need to understand that Jesus cared for others to show his love for God. Jesus wants us to do the same by helping and serving others.

### ACTIVITY

**Followers of Jesus**   Think of people who showed love for others. Mother Teresa showed her love, especially for the poor of India. Dr. Martin Luther King Jr. showed his love for those who were not treated fairly. With your child, make a badge out of construction paper to honor any person you know who follows Jesus. Write the person's name and the words *Follower of Jesus* on the badge.

## WEEKLY PLANNER

### On Sunday

What do today's readings tell you about being a good person? Pick one message from the homily to take home from this week's liturgy.

### On the Web

**www.blestarewe.com**

Visit our Web site for the saint of the day and the reflection question of the week.

### Saint of the Week

 **Saint Vincent de Paul (1581–1660)**

Vincent de Paul lived in France over four hundred years ago. Fr. Vincent fed hungry people, helped them find jobs, and set up clothing collections. He helped build hospitals and children's homes.

**Patron Saint of:** charitable societies
**Feast Day:** September 27

### A Prayer for the Week

Dear Jesus, help us to extend mercy toward others like Saint Vincent de Paul. Let us not pass by anyone in need without helping. Help us to trust as you did, love as you did, and care for others as you did. Amen.

# Take Home

FAMILY TIME

## ✚ Scripture Background

### In the Time of Jesus

**Poverty**   Poverty in the Holy Land was recognized as the result of social factors, such as injustice, rather than a consequence of personal failings. The practice of leaving grain in the fields after harvesting, is described in Ruth 2:2–9. Responsibility for ministering to those who are poor remains fundamental to biblical faith. Jesus himself speaks of the responsibility to assist those in poverty.

You can read of Jesus' approach to poverty and other issues of justice in Matthew 6:1–4, 19:21–26.

## OUR CATHOLIC TRADITION in Literature

### The Seven Storey Mountain

Thomas Merton was a Catholic Trappist monk who died in 1968. He was a convert to Catholicism as a young adult and wrote an autobiography in 1948 about how he moved from atheism to Catholicism. That book, *The Seven Storey Mountain*, became the most famous memoir ever written by an American Catholic. He was a social activist and spoke out on such topics as racial justice, violence, and world peace. His clear vision of how to live a Christian life, his wonderful writing, and his ever-questioning spirit are inspirations for those who have come after him.

# 11 We Act on God's Word

**LET US PRAY** If you believe in me, you will act as
I have acted.

Based on John 14:12

# Share

So many actions
that we take.
We walk and ride.
We bake a cake.

So many actions
every day.
We laugh and smile
We learn and pray.

Imagine yourself in each
picture. What would you do?
Write about an action
you would take.

I would

_____

- - - - - - - - - - - - - - - - - - - - - - - - - - - - -

_____.

I would

_____

- - - - - - - - - - - - - - - - - - - - - - - - - - - - -

_____.

How can
we act on
God's word?

# Hear & Believe

## ✝ Scripture  How Christians Act

Jesus told his followers, "I will return to earth at the end of time. Then I will judge all the people in the world. I will put the people in two groups. To the first group I will say, 'You have done well. I invite you to stay with me forever.' But I will tell the second group, 'Go away. I don't want to see you again.'"

Jesus said that the first group had treated everyone as they would have treated him. They gave food to the hungry. They gave drink to people who were thirsty. They made new people feel at home. They shared their own clothes with people who needed them. They cared for the sick. And they visited people in prison.

The first group of people acted on God's Word. Jesus will welcome them to be with him forever.

Based on Matthew 25:31–46

## Responding in Action

Jesus showed his followers how to live God's Word. He taught people by his words and actions. We show our love for God by how we treat others.

## Our Church Teaches

Jesus told his followers to take care of the needs of others. These actions are called **works of mercy**. When we help others in loving **service**, we act as Jesus did.

### The Works of Mercy

Feed the hungry.

Give drink to the thirsty.

Shelter the homeless.

Give clothing to the poor.

Visit the sick.

Visit those in prison.

Pray for those who have died.

How can we act like Jesus?

# Respond

## Saint Martin de Porres

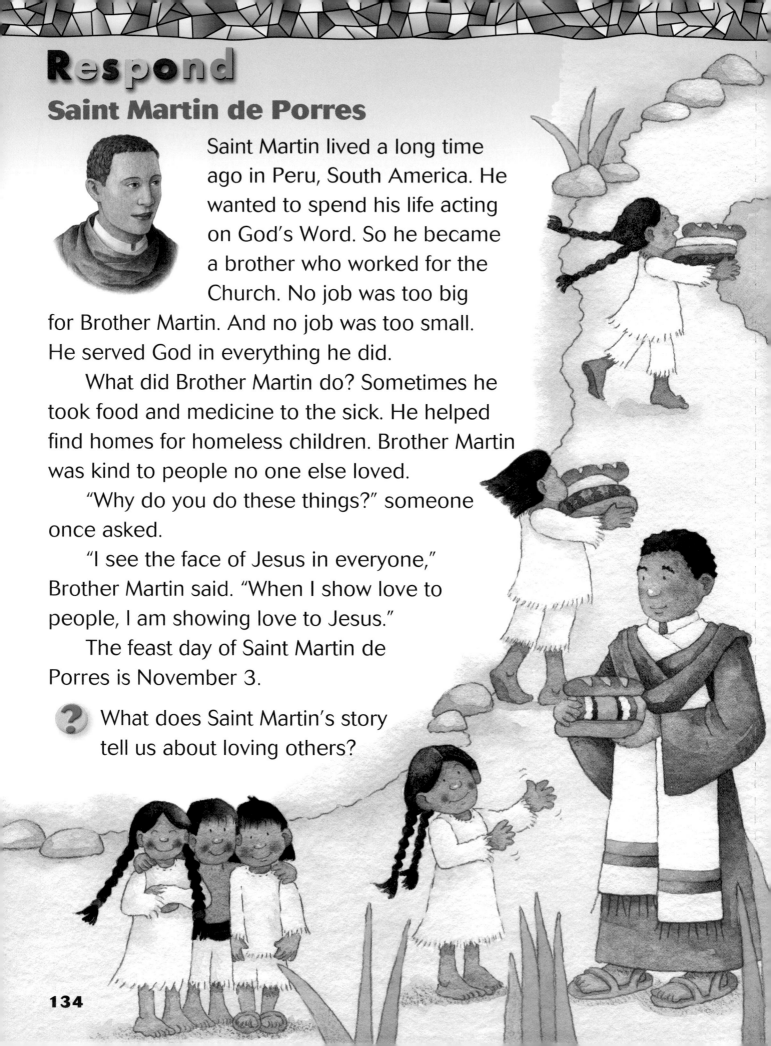

Saint Martin lived a long time ago in Peru, South America. He wanted to spend his life acting on God's Word. So he became a brother who worked for the Church. No job was too big for Brother Martin. And no job was too small. He served God in everything he did.

What did Brother Martin do? Sometimes he took food and medicine to the sick. He helped find homes for homeless children. Brother Martin was kind to people no one else loved.

"Why do you do these things?" someone once asked.

"I see the face of Jesus in everyone," Brother Martin said. "When I show love to people, I am showing love to Jesus."

The feast day of Saint Martin de Porres is November 3.

**?** What does Saint Martin's story tell us about loving others?

# Activity

Follow the directions on the path.

Write one way
that Saint Martin
acted as Jesus did.

_____

- - - - - - - - - - - - - - - - - - - - - -

_____

Draw about a time that
you acted as Jesus did.

Circle one of these works
of mercy that you will try
to do this week.

Visit the sick.
Feed the hungry.

What work of mercy would you
add to the list?

Write it on the sign below.

_____

- - - - - - - - - - - - - - - - - - - - - -

_____

- - - - - - - - - - - - - - - - - - - - - -

_____

How can we
celebrate
acting
on God's
Word?

# Prayer Celebration

## A Listening Prayer

In Italy, Mother Cabrini and her friends taught children. They cared for orphans, and helped the sick. Mother Cabrini later came to the United States. She helped many poor people from Italy. She planned the building of schools, orphanages, and hospitals. Saint Frances Cabrini spent her life acting on God's Word by helping others.

Listen to this prayer. It is part of a prayer that Saint Frances Cabrini wrote.

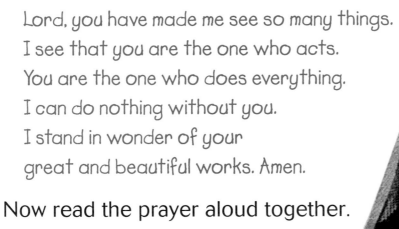

Lord, you have made me see so many things.
I see that you are the one who acts.
You are the one who does everything.
I can do nothing without you.
I stand in wonder of your
great and beautiful works. Amen.

Now read the prayer aloud together.

**A** **Draw** a line to match each need with an action that responds to God's Word.

1. People are hungry.   ●    ● We give them something to drink.

2. People are thirsty.   ●    ● We give them shelter.

3. People are cold.   ●    ● We take care of them.

4. People are sick.   ●    ● We give them clothes.

5. People are homeless.   ●    ● We give them food.

**B** **Complete** each sentence with the correct word.

1. Actions taking care of the needs of _____

   others are works of _____.

2. When we help others in loving ways, _____

   we act as _____ did.

3. People who help others will be with _____

   Jesus _____.

4. Saint Martin de Porres spent his life _____

   acting on God's _____.

| forever |
| Jesus |
| mercy |
| Word |

# Faith in Action

**Youth Ministry** Teens in many parishes belong to a youth ministry. A youth minister leads the group. Teens take part in spiritual and social activities. They find ways to help others in their parish and their community.

## In Your Parish

**Activity** Think about teens who are part of your parish youth ministry. What might you ask them about their group?

## In Everyday Life

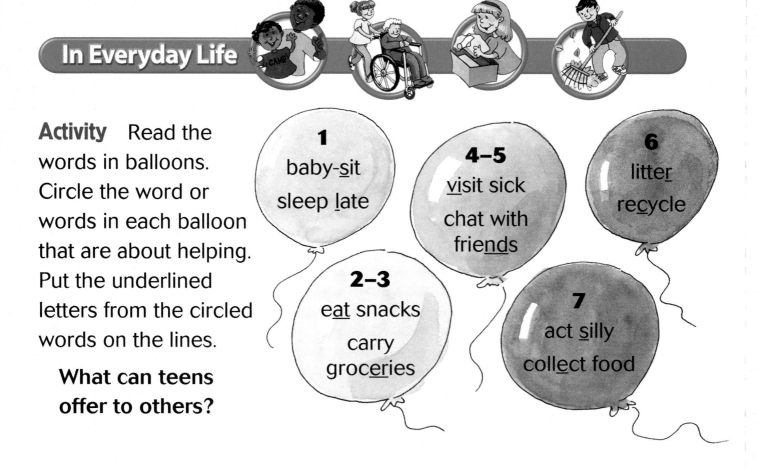

**Activity** Read the words in balloons. Circle the word or words in each balloon that are about helping. Put the underlined letters from the circled words on the lines.

**What can teens offer to others?**

**1** baby-s<u>i</u>t sleep <u>l</u>ate

**4–5** <u>v</u>isit sick chat with fri<u>en</u>ds

**6** litte<u>r</u> re<u>c</u>ycle

**2–3** e<u>at</u> snacks carry groc<u>er</u>ies

**7** act <u>s</u>illy coll<u>ec</u>t food

___  ___  ___  ___  ___  ___  ___
1    2    3    4    5    6    7

# Take Home

FAMILY TIME

# We Pray for Others

In this chapter, children will become more aware of the needs of others. Sometimes all we can do to help others is to pray for them. The children will come to realize that, when we pray, we trust God to care for people's needs. The children will also compose their own prayers for other people.

### ACTIVITY

**Trust Walk**   Blindfold one family member. Then have someone be the trust-walk leader. It is the leader's job to make sure that the blindfolded person doesn't bump into anything or get hurt. It is the blindfolded person's job to trust the leader. Take turns being the blindfolded person and the leader. Then talk about what it was like to play these roles.

## WEEKLY PLANNER

### On Sunday

Listen for the priest to say the words "Let us pray." When he pauses, use the opportunity to be quiet and prayerful.

### On the Web

**www.blestarewe.com**

Visit our Web site for the saint of the day and the reflection question of the week.

### Saint of the Week

**Saint Paula Montal Fornés (1799–1889)**

Paula was born in Spain. After her father died, she worked as a seamstress to help her family. With a friend she began a school. She later founded the Daughters of Mary. She was canonized in 2001.

**Patron Saint of:** seamstresses
**Feast Day:** February 26

A Prayer for the Week

Lord, sometimes we are caught up with our own needs and we ignore the needs of those around us. Open our hearts to see the needs of others as did Saint Paula Montal Fornés. Amen.

# Getting ready for Chapter 12

## Take Home

## ✝ Scripture Background

### In the Time of Jesus

**Prayer** The earliest instances of prayer recorded in the Old Testament are conversations God initiates with people. In Genesis, God speaks with Adam (1:28–30), and with Abraham (15:1–21). In Exodus 3:4–22, God speaks with Moses. Christ's role as mediator between God and humans is shown in the New Testament. Prayer is addressed to God through Jesus Christ. This is based on the concept that God's grace and love come through Christ.

You can read of Jesus' role as mediator in John 1:1–18.

## OUR CATHOLIC TRADITION in Prayer

**Novenas** *Do not despise my poor prayer. Do not let my trust be confounded!*

This prayer is part of a novena to Saint Jude. Also known as Saint Jude Thaddeus, he is the patron saint of impossible causes.

A novena is a repeated prayer asking for a specific intention. *Novena* comes from the Latin word *novem*, or *nine*. It reflects the Apostles' experience. They prayed for nine days awaiting the Holy Spirit at Pentecost. Most novenas are prayed for nine days in a row, or once weekly for nine weeks. They may be made to saints, angels, and even God. Mary is perhaps most often addressed in novenas.

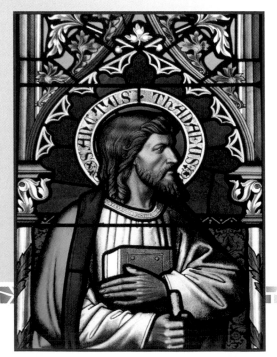

# 12 We Pray for Others

**O God, hear me and answer my prayer.**

Based on Psalm 17:6

## Share

Have you ever made a list of things you wish you could do? You might want to learn to ice skate. Maybe you would like to see the ocean.

Write three of your wishes here.

### My Wish List

1. I wish _____.

2. I wish _____.

3. I wish _____.

What do church members ask for when they pray?

# Hear & Believe

## ✝ Scripture  Jesus and Prayer

Jesus taught about kinds of prayer. He said we should ask God for what we need for ourselves. "Ask, and you shall receive," Jesus said. "Pray for what you need, and God will give it to you."

Jesus also asked us to pray for the needs of other people. "When you come together to pray for others, I will be with you," Jesus promised. "God will give you whatever you ask for in my name."

On the night before he died, Jesus ate a special meal with his friends. This meal is called the **Last Supper**. Jesus blessed bread and wine. He shared it with his friends. Then Jesus prayed for them. "Father, please help my friends in their work. Help them tell others about your love."

Based on Matthew 7:7–8; John 16:23; 17:9–21

142

## Kinds of Prayer

Jesus told his friends to place their trust in God. When we pray for ourselves, we know that God will answer us. When we pray for other people, we trust that God will care for them, too.

## Our Church Teaches

We ask God the Father to help us be good followers of Jesus. We pray for the needs of others at Mass. The Liturgy of the Word ends with the **Prayer of the Faithful**. In this prayer, we pray for people everywhere.

## We Believe

We trust our heavenly Father to answer our prayers. We know that God gives us what is truly good for us.

## Faith Words

**Prayer of the Faithful**
The Prayer of the Faithful is the last part of the Liturgy of the Word at Mass. We pray for the needs of people everywhere.

How can we pray for others?

# Respond

## The Needs of Others

Before we can pray for others, we need to know what they need. The photos on this page tell stories. Talk about what the people need.

 How would you ask God to care for these people?

144

# Activities

The prayer below is a prayer for people in need.

> For those who are sick,
> we pray to the Lord.

**1.** Use your own words to complete these prayers for other people.

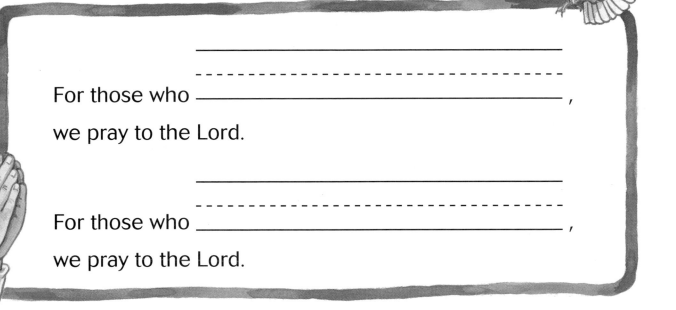

For those who _____ ,

we pray to the Lord.

For those who _____ ,

we pray to the Lord.

**2.** Color each space that has an **X**. What is the hidden message?

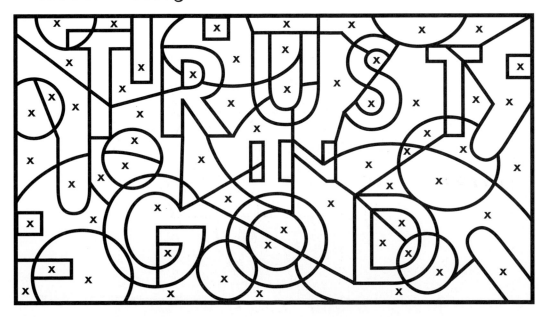

How can we celebrate a Prayer of the Faithful?

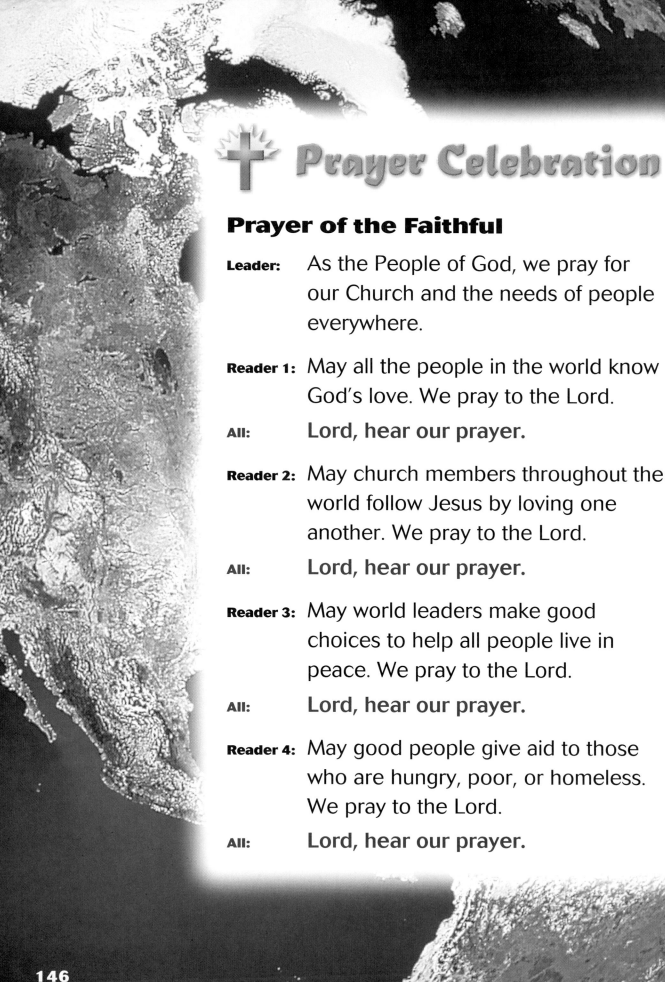

## ✝ Prayer Celebration

## Prayer of the Faithful

**Leader:** As the People of God, we pray for our Church and the needs of people everywhere.

**Reader 1:** May all the people in the world know God's love. We pray to the Lord.

**All:** Lord, hear our prayer.

**Reader 2:** May church members throughout the world follow Jesus by loving one another. We pray to the Lord.

**All:** Lord, hear our prayer.

**Reader 3:** May world leaders make good choices to help all people live in peace. We pray to the Lord.

**All:** Lord, hear our prayer.

**Reader 4:** May good people give aid to those who are hungry, poor, or homeless. We pray to the Lord.

**All:** Lord, hear our prayer.

**A** **Respond** to the following question.

Who is it that God the Father wants us to follow?

_____

- - - - - - - - - - - - - - - - - - - - - - - - - - - - - - - -

_____

**B** **Circle** the best answers to complete the sentences.

1. Jesus celebrated the _____ with his friends.

   **Last Supper**　　**lesson**　　**Mass**

2. Jesus taught about kinds of _____.

   **Mass**　　　　**prayer**　　　**salad**

3. During the _____ we pray for people everywhere.

   **Nicene Creed**　　**Prayer of the Faithful**
   **Rosary**

4. We _____ God to answer our prayers.

   **doubt**　　　　**trust**　　　　**wish**

5. The Liturgy of the _____ ends with the Prayer of the Faithful.

   **Eucharist**　　　**Mass**　　　　**Word**

# Faith in Action

**Prayer Groups**  Some adults come together in prayer groups to praise and thank God. They read and talk about the Bible. Some groups pray for healing and peace. Some meet to pray the Rosary. They pray for their children and people in need.

### In Everyday Life

**Activity**  Think of times when you pray together with other people. What do you pray for with others?

### In Your Parish

**Activity**  Find these words about prayer groups:

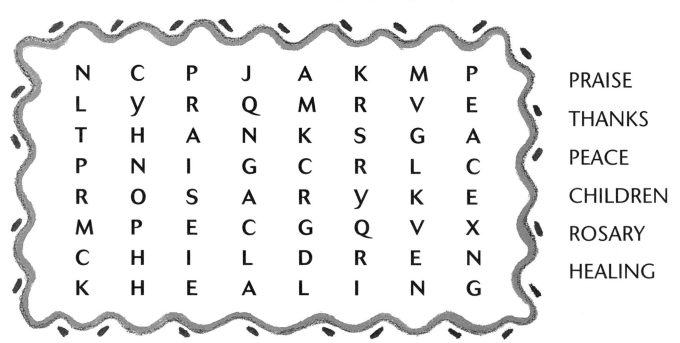

| N | C | P | J | A | K | M | P |
|---|---|---|---|---|---|---|---|
| L | y | R | Q | M | R | V | E |
| T | H | A | N | K | S | G | A |
| P | N | I | G | C | R | L | C |
| R | O | S | A | R | y | K | E |
| M | P | E | C | G | Q | V | X |
| C | H | I | L | D | R | E | N |
| K | H | E | A | L | I | N | G |

PRAISE

THANKS

PEACE

CHILDREN

ROSARY

HEALING

# We Celebrate the Gift of Eucharist

God's greatest gift to us is his only Son, Jesus Christ. We celebrate the Eucharist to praise and thank God for this gift. We celebrate to share more fully in the life of Christ.

*I am the bread of life. Those who eat this bread will never be hungry.*
Based on John 6:35

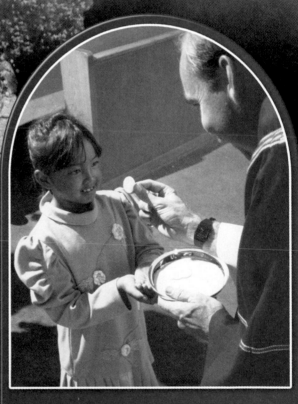

Jesus was buried in a tomb very much like the one shown here. We remember Jesus' death and Resurrection each time we receive Holy Communion.

# Eat This Bread

John 6, Adapted by Robert J. Batastini and the Taizé Community

Music by Jacques Berthier

**REFRAIN**

Eat this bread, drink this cup, come to him and nev-er be hun-gry.

Eat this bread, drink this cup, trust in him and you will not thirst.

© 1984, Les Presses de Taizé, GIA Publications, Inc., agent.

# Take Home

FAMILY TIME

# Jesus Saves Us from Sin

We know that Jesus gave up his life to save all of us from sin. We all share the benefit of his great sacrifice. This chapter presents the story of Jesus' death and Resurrection. Children will consider the concept of sacrifice as it applies to everyday life, and they will learn about the ultimate sacrifice Jesus made when he gave up his life so that we could be saved from sin.

**ACTIVITY**

**The Rugged Cross** Together, make a cross of twigs held together with a piece of twine or a pipe cleaner. Display your work in a prominent place. Let it serve as a reminder that Jesus sacrificed his life to save us from sin.

## WEEKLY PLANNER

### On Sunday
After the consecration, say (or sing) the words "Christ has died, Christ is risen, Christ will come again" with a new sense of appreciation.

### On the Web
**www.blestarewe.com**

Visit our Web site for the saint of the day and the reflection question of the week.

### Saint of the Week

**Saint Elizabeth of Hungary** (1207–1231)
Elizabeth was born a princess in Hungary. She and her husband loved their four children. After her husband died, she raised the children alone. She later joined the Third Order of Saint Francis.

**Patron Saint of:** homeless people and exiles
**Feast Day:** November 17

**A Prayer for the Week**

Jesus, help us to be like Saint Elizabeth making sacrifices to care for others. Our efforts will be a way to thank you for your great sacrifice. You gave up your life to save us. Amen.

FAMILY TIME

## ✝ Scripture Background

### In the Time of Jesus

**Crucifixion** The "most wretched of deaths," crucifixion, was reserved for criminals involved in serious crimes. It was an act of treason for Jesus to be considered a king, thus meriting crucifixion in the eyes of first-century Romans. The letters of Paul, however, identify the cross as a symbol of victory. By it, we have been set free and redeemed from the power of sin.

You can read of Jesus' crucifixion in Mark 15:22–29, and Paul's interpretation of it in 1 Corinthians 1:19–27.

# OUR CATHOLIC TRADITION in World Ministries

### Congregation of Holy Cross

Father Basil Anthony Moreau sought to be a true disciple of Jesus. A priest, he was born in 1799, near the end of the French Revolution. There was a need for ministry in France. Father Moreau gathered a group of priests and brothers to establish the Congregation of Holy Cross in 1837. Today four congregations follow his spirit and ministry: the Congregation of Holy Cross, the Marianites of Holy Cross, the Sisters of the Holy Cross, and Sisters of Holy Cross. They minister worldwide. In 2003, Pope John Paul II named Fr. Basil Moreau "Venerable," a first step toward sainthood.

# 13 Jesus Saves Us from Sin

The greatest love you can show is to give up your life for your friends.

Based on John 15:13

## Share

Acting on God's Word is not always easy. Sometimes we have to give up what we want. Sometimes we have to put the needs of others first.

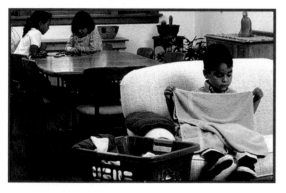

**What is the boy giving up? Why is he doing this?**

**What is the girl giving up? Why is she doing this?**

Draw a picture that shows a time when you gave up something.

What did Jesus give up for us?

# Hear & Believe

## ✝ Scripture  Jesus Gives Up His Life

Jesus gave up his life to save us from sin. Jesus was arrested the night he shared a special meal with his friends. The next morning, soldiers gave Jesus a wooden cross to carry. Then they put Jesus to death on the cross.

After Jesus died, some of his friends took his body away. They placed his body in a tomb.

Three days later, some women friends went to the tomb. When they got there, the tomb was empty. An angel told the friends that Jesus had been raised from the dead.

Based on Mark 14:46; 15:16–47; 16:1–6

## God's Gift of Jesus

Jesus is God the Father's greatest gift to us. Jesus gave up his life as a **sacrifice** for our sins. A sacrifice is a special gift that is given out of love.

We call Jesus our **Savior**. A savior rescues others from danger. Jesus died on the cross to save us from our sins.

## Our Church Teaches

Three days after Jesus' death, God raised Jesus to new life. By his life, death and **Resurrection**, Jesus showed us God's love. We received the promise of new life. On Easter we celebrate Jesus' Resurrection.

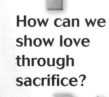

How can we show love through sacrifice?

# Respond

## Saint Elizabeth of Hungary

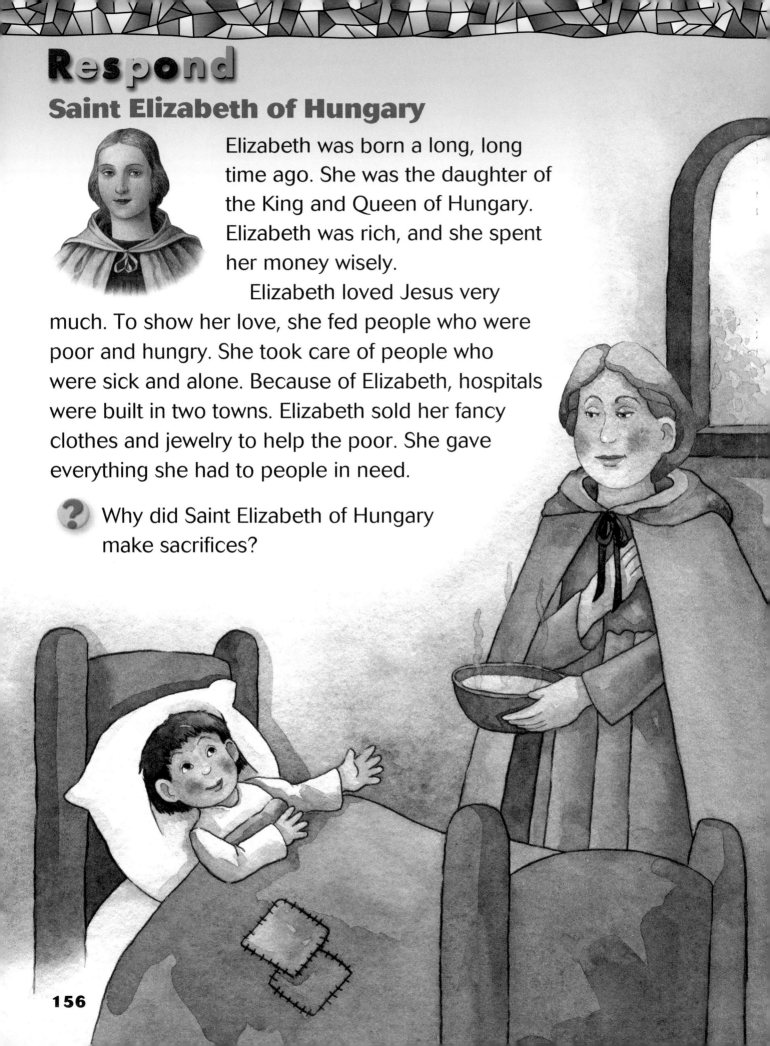

Elizabeth was born a long, long time ago. She was the daughter of the King and Queen of Hungary. Elizabeth was rich, and she spent her money wisely.

Elizabeth loved Jesus very much. To show her love, she fed people who were poor and hungry. She took care of people who were sick and alone. Because of Elizabeth, hospitals were built in two towns. Elizabeth sold her fancy clothes and jewelry to help the poor. She gave everything she had to people in need.

**?** Why did Saint Elizabeth of Hungary make sacrifices?

# Activities

1. Think of one loving thing you could do this week. Write about how this sacrifice will show your love for someone.

   _____

   - - - - - - - - - - - - - - - - - - - - - - - -

   _____

   _____

   - - - - - - - - - - - - - - - - - - - - - - - -

   _____

   _____

   - - - - - - - - - - - - - - - - - - - - - - - -

   _____

2. At Mass we listen as the priest prays, "Let us proclaim the mystery of faith."

   Trace over the dotted words below. You will find "the mystery of faith."

   Lord, by your cross

   and Resurrection

   you have set us

   free. You are the

   Savior of the world.

How can we celebrate the sacrifice of Jesus?

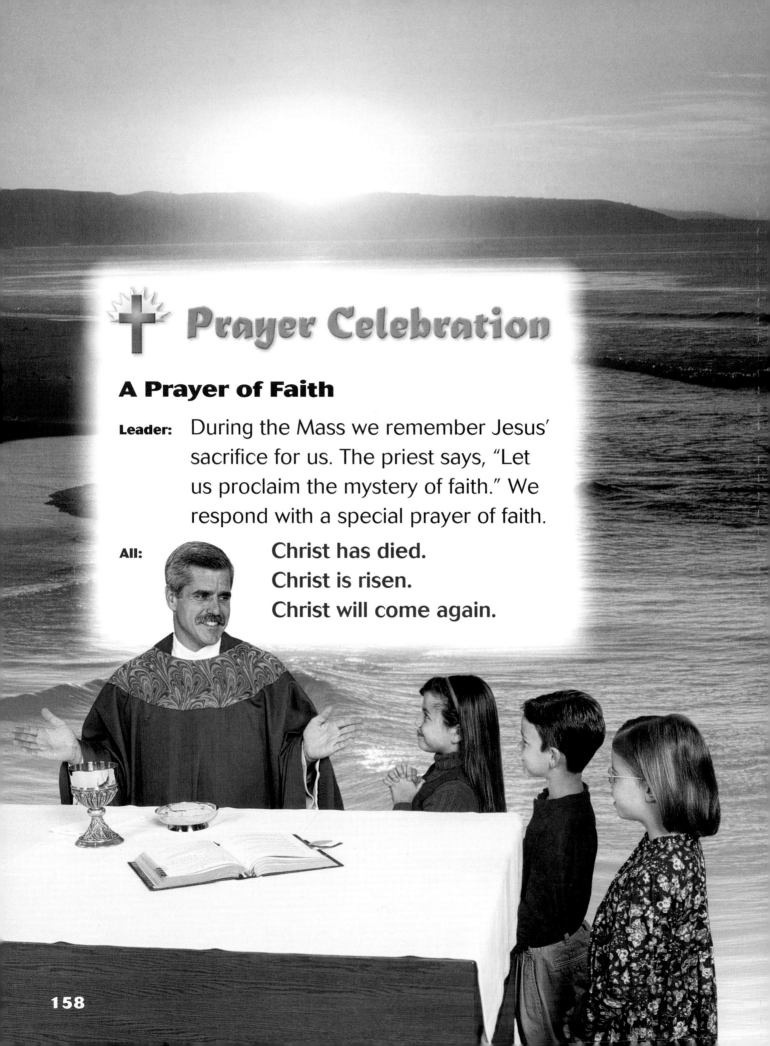

# ✝ Prayer Celebration

## A Prayer of Faith

**Leader:** During the Mass we remember Jesus' sacrifice for us. The priest says, "Let us proclaim the mystery of faith." We respond with a special prayer of faith.

**All:** Christ has died.
Christ is risen.
Christ will come again.

**A** **Draw a line** to connect the parts of each sentence.

1. Giving up something we want out of love is _____

2. Jesus is God the Father's _____

3. A savior _____

• rescues others from danger.

• called a sacrifice.

• greatest gift to us.

**B** **Complete** the sentences with words from the box.

come      died      Jesus      risen

_____

1. During Mass, we remember that _____ died and was raised from the dead.

2. Complete this prayer from the Mass.

_____

"Christ has _____,

_____

Christ is _____,

_____

Christ will _____ again."

# Faith in Action

**Culture Club** Some families belong to a culture club in their parish. In this club, they learn about people from other cultures. Club members choose a culture and read favorite stories from it. They learn about types of clothing people may wear for special occasions. They sing songs in different languages. Sometimes the families share foods from different cultures together.

**In Your Parish**

**Activity** Think about people who have visited or joined your parish from other places. From what states or countries did they come?

**In Everyday Life**

**Activity** Unscramble the words below. Use them to finish the sentence.

LAL                          KETA

We ____ ____ ____ are called to ____ ____ ____ ____

ERCA                         OHTRE

____ ____ ____ ____ of each ____ ____ ____ ____ ____.

# Take Home

FAMILY TIME

# We Receive the Gift of Jesus

Some gifts are so great that we remember them for a lifetime. Other gifts, such as fresh air and clean water, we hardly give any thought to at all. This chapter presents the concept of Jesus in the Eucharist as gift.

Children will learn that we remember the Last Supper at Mass. They will discover that Jesus is present in the bread and wine. Lastly, they will learn how to receive Jesus in the Eucharist.

## ACTIVITY

**It's All Set** Teach your child how to set the table. Show where to put the plates, glasses, napkins, and silverware. If possible, put candles and flowers on the table. Explain that, just as the altar is set in a particular way for Mass, so the family table should be set for a meal.

## WEEKLY PLANNER

### On Sunday

Listen carefully to the words of consecration. As you receive Communion, think about what you have heard.

### On the Web

**www.blestarewe.com**

Visit our Web site for the saint of the day and the reflection question of the week.

### Saint of the Week

**Saint Teresa of the Andes** (1900–1920)

Juanita was born in Chile. She took the name Teresa of Jesus as a Carmelite nun. She soon became sick with typhoid fever and died. In 1993, she became the first Chilean to be canonized.

**Patron Saint of:** sick people and all young people
**Feast Day:** July 13

### A Prayer for the Week

O Lord, we give thanks for the great gift of Eucharist. We recognize the Eucharist as Jesus' greatest gift. May we share all our gifts with others. Amen.

# Take Home

FAMILY TIME

## ✚ Scripture Background

### In the Time of Jesus

**Passover Meal**   Jesus' Last Supper was a Passover meal to commemorate freedom of Jews from Egyptian slavery. Foods at this meal have special meaning. The Matzo, or unleavened bread, represents manna which fed the Israelites in the desert; bitter herbs symbolize the harshness of slavery; the lamb recalls the sacrifice at the first Passover; and the egg symbolizes new life in the covenant with God.

You can read about Jesus' Last Supper in Matthew 26:17–30.

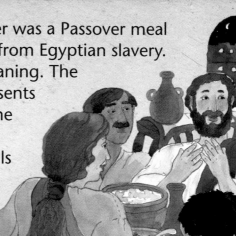

# OUR CATHOLIC TRADITION in Music

*Jesus Christ Superstar*   is a rock opera about the life of Christ with music by Andrew Lloyd Webber and lyrics by Tim Rice. The story is about the last week of Jesus' life, and it tells about the guilt Judas experiences when he betrays Jesus. The scene that depicts the Last Supper recreates the relationship of Jesus with the Twelve Apostles.

   Originally performed on Broadway in 1971, the show ran from 1972 to 1980 in London. It opened on Broadway again in April, 2000. *Jesus Christ Superstar*, the first musical to incorporate rock music, gives us an opportunity to take a new look at a very familiar story and think about it in a fresh way.

# 14 We Receive the Gift of Jesus

**LET US PRAY** I am the bread of life. Those who come to me will never be hungry.

Based on John 6:35

# Share

We all need food and water to stay healthy. But we have other needs, or hungers, too. Look at these pictures. How is each person hungry?

Rosemary is very, very tired. She is hungry for

———————————————

– – – – – – – – – – – – – – – – – – – – – – – – – –

—————————————— .

Matt has not eaten since lunch. He is hungry for

———————————————

– – – – – – – – – – – – – – – – – – – – – – –

——————————— .

Luis can't rake all these leaves. He is hungry for

———————————————

– – – – – – – – – – – – – – – – – – – – – – –

——————————— .

How does Jesus answer our needs and hungers?

# Hear & Believe

##  Worship  The Gift of Eucharist

The second part of Mass is the **Liturgy of the Eucharist**. We offer gifts of bread and wine. We remember the Last Supper. The priest prepares the gifts for the celebration of Eucharist. He prays:

On the night before he died for us,
Jesus had a special supper with his friends.
He took bread and gave thanks to God
his Father. He broke the bread and
gave it to his friends, saying:
  "Take this, all of you, and eat it:
  this is my body which will be
  given up for you."
In the same way he took a cup of wine.
He gave thanks to God and
handed the cup to his friends,
saying:
  "Take this, all of you,
  and drink from it: this is
  the cup of my blood. It will
  be shed for you and for all so
  that sins may be forgiven."
Then he said to them,
  "Do this in memory of me."

Based on Eucharistic Prayer for
Masses with Children III

## The Meal of God's People

During Mass we remember Jesus' Last Supper. At that meal, Jesus changed bread and wine into his Body and Blood. At Mass we also remember the death and Resurrection of Jesus Christ.

The Mass is a holy meal for the People of God today. At Mass Jesus gives us himself in the **Eucharist**. We give thanks for Jesus' sacrifice. Through the Holy Spirit bread and wine become the Body and Blood of Jesus Christ.

GO TO pages 269–270 to learn more about the Liturgy of the Eucharist.

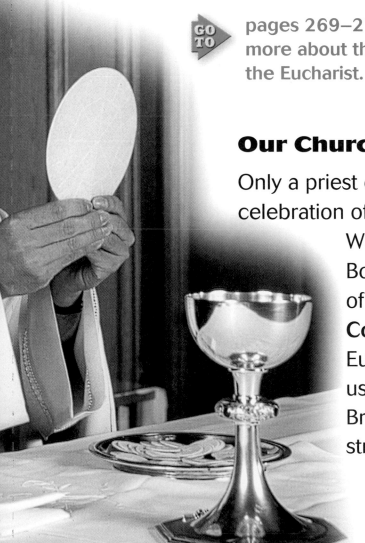

### Our Church Teaches

Only a priest can lead the celebration of the Eucharist. We receive the Body and Blood of Christ in **Holy Communion**. The Eucharist unites us with Jesus, the Bread of Life. He strengthens us.

**We Believe**

Christ is present in the bread and wine at Mass. In them, Christ gives us himself, the Bread of Life.

**Faith Words**

**Eucharist**
The Eucharist is a sacrifice and a special meal of thanks. We receive the Body and Blood of Christ.

How do church members receive Communion?

165

# Respond

## Going to Communion

Mr. Wills was teaching religion to a group of girls and boys. He said, "Tell me what you know about receiving Communion."

Every hand in the group shot up!

Paolo answered first. "I must have already received Reconciliation before my First Communion. I must be free of serious sin," he said.

Lucy said, "I shouldn't eat or drink anything but water for one hour before receiving Communion."

"I can receive Communion either in my hand or on my tongue," added April.

"The priest, deacon, or extraordinary minister of Holy Communion says the **Body of Christ**. Then I bow and answer **Amen**," said Mike.

Kye added, "I also say **Amen** when I hear the **Blood of Christ** if I receive from the cup."

Then Buddy said, "After Communion, I return to my place in church. I give thanks because I have received the gift of Eucharist."

"Wow!" said Mr. Wills. "You didn't forget a thing!"

**?** What do you do after receiving Communion?

# Activity

Where you see a **Q**, an **X**, or a **Z** in the puzzle, cross it out.

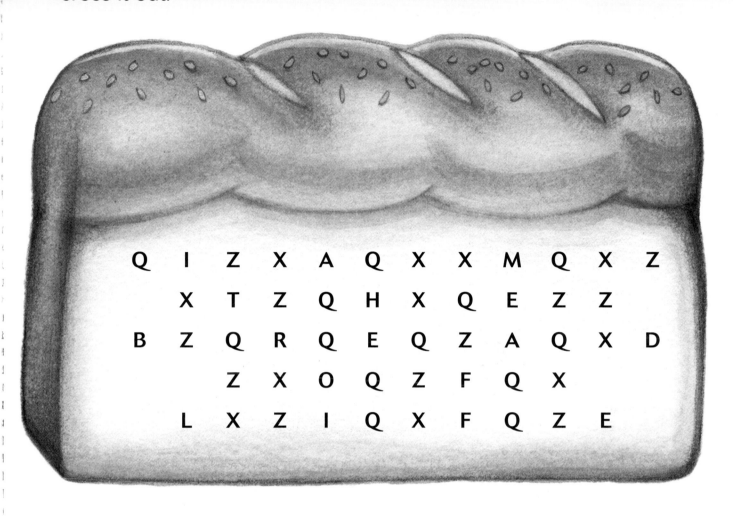

Q I Z X A Q X X M Q X Z
X T Z Q H X Q E Z Z
B Z Q R Q E Q Z A Q X D
Z X O Q Z F Q X
L X Z I Q X F Q Z E

Write the sentence you found in the puzzle.

_____

- - - - - - - - - - - - - - - - - - - - - - - - - - - -

_____

_____

- - - - - - - - - - - - - - - - - - - - - - - - - - - -

_____

_____

- - - - - - - - - - - - - - - - - - - - - - - - - - - -

_____ .

**How can we celebrate being one with Jesus?**

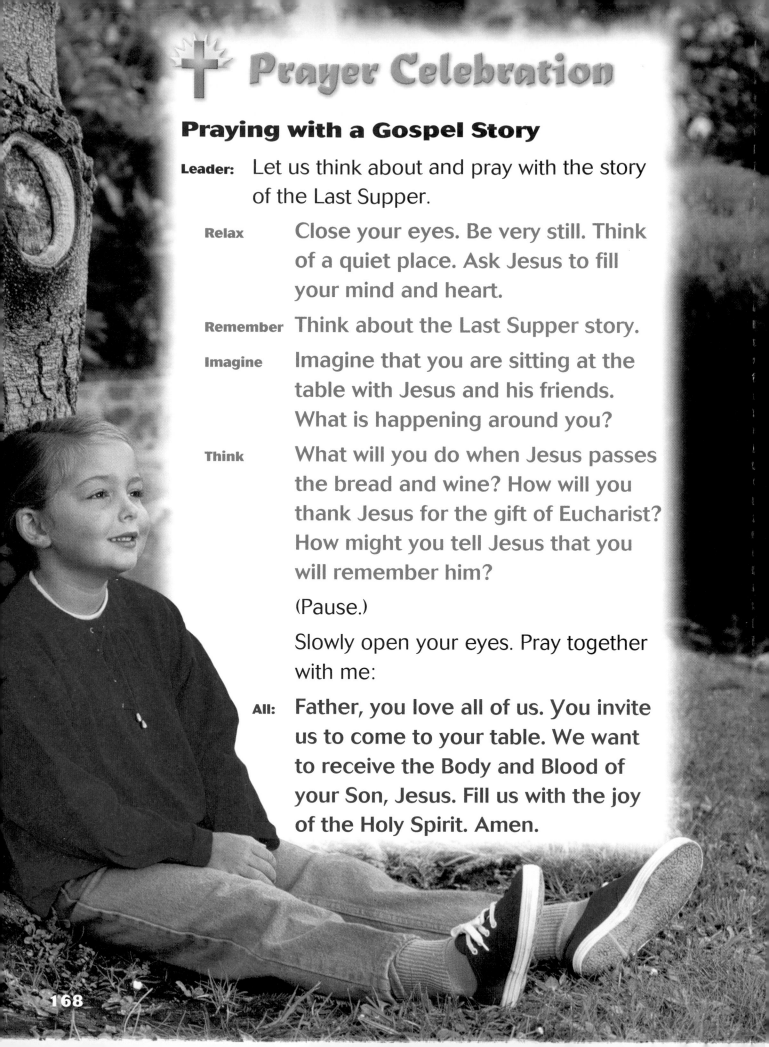

# ✝ Prayer Celebration

## Praying with a Gospel Story

**Leader:** Let us think about and pray with the story of the Last Supper.

**Relax** Close your eyes. Be very still. Think of a quiet place. Ask Jesus to fill your mind and heart.

**Remember** Think about the Last Supper story.

**Imagine** Imagine that you are sitting at the table with Jesus and his friends. What is happening around you?

**Think** What will you do when Jesus passes the bread and wine? How will you thank Jesus for the gift of Eucharist? How might you tell Jesus that you will remember him?

(Pause.)

Slowly open your eyes. Pray together with me:

**All:** Father, you love all of us. You invite us to come to your table. We want to receive the Body and Blood of your Son, Jesus. Fill us with the joy of the Holy Spirit. Amen.

**A** **Complete** the definition.

The Eucharist is a sacrifice and a special meal of

_____

- - - - - - - - - - - - - - - - - - - - - - - - - - - - - - - -

_____.

**B** **Draw** a line to match the descriptions with the correct words.

1. Another name for receiving the Body of Christ     ●    ● in the hand

2. Our answer when the minister of Communion says, "The Body of Christ"     ●    ● Last Supper

3. One way to receive Holy Communion     ●    ● Amen

4. Who presides, or leads, the Eucharist     ●    ● Holy Communion

5. What we remember during the Liturgy of the Eucharist     ●    ● priest

# Faith in Action

**Extraordinary Ministers of Holy Communion** During Mass, extraordinary ministers of Holy Communion help give out Communion. These people show respect for each person they serve. They also bring the gift of Christ to people who are homebound and pray with them.

## In Everyday Life

**Activity** Model a way of showing respect when handing out papers or books to others.

## In Your Parish

**Activity** Write the letter for the missing word in each sentence.

| **A** Eucharist | **B** gift | **C** priests | **D** respect | **E** serve |
| --- | --- | --- | --- | --- |

**1.** All who give out Communion show _____ for others.

**2.** Deacons and _____ also give Communion.

**3.** Ministers of Communion bring the _____ to others.

**4.** All ministers of Communion _____ people.

**5.** In Eucharist, we receive the _____ of Christ.

# We Carry On the Work of Jesus

Chapter 15 presents the New Commandment that Jesus gave us about loving one another. Children will discover how Jesus showed his love for people. They will also identify ways that they can show their love for others.

## ACTIVITY

**Choose One** With your child's help, think of different tasks any family member could do, such as put away toys or fold towels. Together, write the tasks on slips of paper, fold them, and place them in a bowl. Then have each person take one slip from the bowl each day and complete the task.

## WEEKLY PLANNER

### On Sunday

As you pray silently during the prayer after Communion, reflect on how you will love others as Jesus loves you.

### On the Web

**www.blestarewe.com**

Visit our Web site for the saint of the day and the reflection question of the week.

### Saint of the Week

**Blessed Marianne of Molokai** (1838–1918)

Barbara Cope was born in Germany. She took the name Marianne as a nun. She joined Father Damien on the Island of Molokai. Mother Marianne worked with young leper patients. She was beatified in 2005.

**Patron Saint of:** victims of leprosy, AIDS
**Feast Day:** January 23

### A Prayer for the Week

Through her works, Lord, Mother Marianne shared your love with others. Help us carry on good works with acts of kindness, healing, and love. Amen.

# Take Home

FAMILY TIME

## ✝ Scripture Background

### In the Time of Jesus

**Illness and Sin** For centuries, the Israelites believed that illness or affliction was punishment from God for having sinned. The evil actions of groups were thought to bring about natural calamities, plagues, or misfortune. Jesus rejected such connections. However, Jesus often linked healing someone with the forgiveness of that person's sins to show God's power over both body and soul.

You can read of Jesus' healing powers in Mark 5:21–42.

## OUR CATHOLIC TRADITION in Religious Life

**Blessed Damien de Veuster**
Damien de Veuster was a holy person who risked his life caring for others. Born in Belgium in 1840, he joined the Sacred Heart Fathers as a young man. After ordination to the priesthood, he served in the Hawaiian missions. In 1866, a sickness known as leprosy spread across the Hawaiian Islands. Lepers were exiled to the Island of Molokai. Father Damien volunteered to minister to them. He took care of them, built houses, hospitals, and churches. He contracted leprosy in 1885 and died in 1889. Pope John Paul II beatified Damien de Veuster In 1995.

# 15 We Carry On the Work of Jesus

**Love one another as I have loved you.**

Based on John 13:34

# Share

What kind of workers do you see?

What kind of work would you like to do when you grow up? Show it in a drawing.

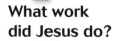
**What work did Jesus do?**

# Hear & Believe

## ✝ Scripture  Jesus and the Little Girl

**Storyteller:** One day Jesus was speaking to a crowd of people. A man named Jairus was there.

**Jairus:** (kneels in front of Jesus) Lord, please come to my home. Please help my sick daughter.

**Jesus:** Show me the way. I will help her.

**Jairus:** (gets up) Thank you, Jesus. Let's go!

**Storyteller:** They started walking. A servant from the house of Jairus ran up to them.

**Servant:** Sir, your daughter just died.

**Storyteller:** Jairus was very sad.

**Jesus:** Do not be afraid, Jairus. Believe that I can help.

**Storyteller:** When they got to the house, Jesus went in. The dead girl was lying on the bed.

**Jesus:** (taking her hand) Little girl, get up!

**Storyteller:** The little girl got up at once. She hugged her father.

**Jairus:** Jesus, how can I ever thank you?

**Jesus:** Try to love everyone as I have loved you.

Based on Mark 5:21–24, 35–42

## The Work of Jesus

In this Bible story, Jesus showed his love for Jairus and his daughter. Jesus taught people about God's love for everyone. He did this in many ways. He told stories. He shared food. He forgave sinners. He comforted sad people. Jesus healed the sick. He even brought dead people back to life.

## Our Church Teaches

In the **New Commandment** Jesus said, "Love one another as I have loved you." This is the law of love. We are called to love others the way God loves us. We live by Jesus' law of love. We do this when we show our love for others.

### We Believe
When we love others, we are following Jesus. We are also showing our love for God.

### Faith Words
**New Commandment**
The New Commandment from Jesus is, "Love one another as I have loved you."

What are some ordinary ways we can love others?

# Respond

## Taking Care of Others

"Mrs. Nye wasn't at Mass Sunday," said Mattie. "She is home, sick and alone. She can't even cook!

"Everybody wanted to help. Dr. Ray stopped in to see Mrs. Nye. Joey Garcia brought her a nice lunch. He stayed and visited for a while. The Grant family prepared her dinner."

"So that took care of Sunday. What about the rest of the week?" asked Kim.

Mattie answered, "Parish members will take meals to Mrs. Nye every day."

"Let's ask everybody in the parish to pray for her, too, " added Kim.

"You know, Jesus taught us to love one another as he loved us. When we care for Mrs. Nye, we show our love for God!"

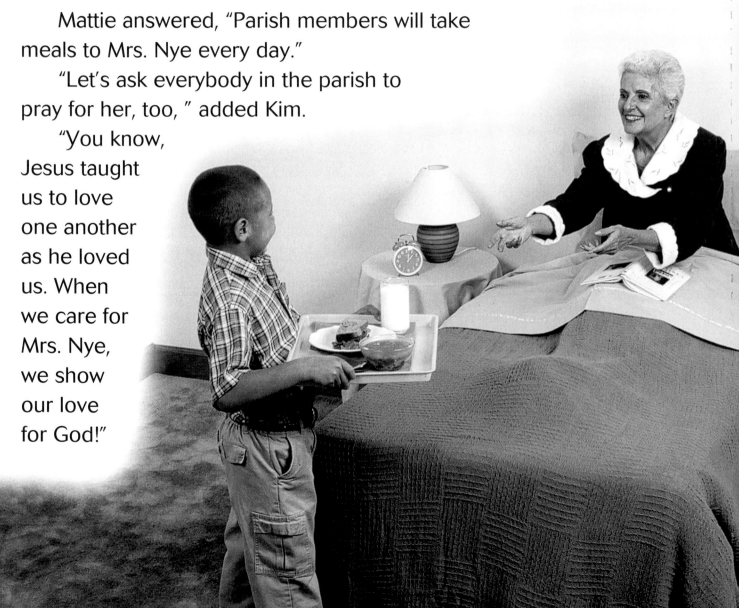

# Activities

Show how you can carry on the work of Jesus.

**1.** Write four words you can say to someone who is sad.

_____     _____

- - - - - - - - - - - - - - - - - - - - - - - - -     - - - - - - - - - - - - - - - - - - - - - - - - -

_____     _____

_____     _____

- - - - - - - - - - - - - - - - - - - - - - - - -     - - - - - - - - - - - - - - - - - - - - - - - - -

_____     _____

**2.** Draw a picture that shows how you can help a sick person.

How can we pray a simple prayer for others?

# Prayer Celebration

## A Thumb Prayer for Others

You can pray for others by using just your thumb. Trace a small Sign of the Cross with your thumb. On the downward stroke of the cross, think "Jesus." On the sideways stroke, think the name of someone you are praying for.

You might pray ⬇ "Jesus," then ➡ "Uncle Jim." Trace your thumb cross in the palm of your hand, on a book, or anywhere.

Choose one of the thumb prayers below. Say your prayer over and over.

⬇ Jesus ➡ the Pope

⬇ Jesus ➡ all parents

⬇ Jesus ➡ those in need

⬇ Jesus ➡ our pastor

⬇ Jesus ➡ all children

⬇ Jesus ➡ (your own prayer)

**A** **Circle** the best answer.

1. How can we follow Jesus?
   **We can fight.**     **We can show love.**     **We can sin.**

2. "Love one another as I have loved you." What do we call this law?
   **Ten Commandments**     **New Commandment**     **Creed**

3. Who did Jesus forgive?
   **dead people**     **sad people**     **sinful people**

4. In the Thumb Prayer, what sign do you make?
   **Sign of the Cross**     **Sign of Peace**     **Stop Sign**

**B** **Draw or write** about ways to love others as Jesus did.

# Faith in Action

**Parish Nurse** Many parishes have a parish nurse. This person serves the whole parish community. The nurse helps people find health services. This nurse visits the sick to help them heal. Some parish nurses teach classes on health care. People share their concerns with a parish nurse. By praying together they grow in faith.

**In Your Parish**

**Activity** Use the code to write the missing letters.

A B C D E F G H I L N O R S T
1 2 3 4 5 6 7 8 9 10 11 12 13 14 15

**A parish nurse helps people with**

__ __ __ __ H , H __ __ __ __ __ H ,
6 1 9 15 8    8 5 1 10 15 8

and H __ __ __ __ __ __ .
8 5 1 10 9 11 7

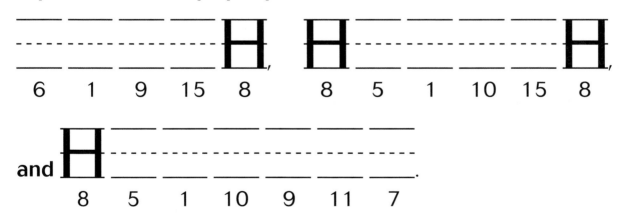

**In Everyday Life**

**Activity** Think about the nurse that visits your school. In what ways does a school nurse help students?

FAMILY TIME

# We Pray Like Jesus

We call God "our Father" because Jesus asked us to, and we pray the Lord's Prayer because Jesus taught it to us. In Chapter 16, children learn to pray the Lord's Prayer with an understanding of its meaning. The children will also identify the parts of the day in which they might pray.

## ACTIVITY

**Daily Bread** The bread that we eat every day may be very different from the bread Jesus ate, or from the breads eaten in other parts of the world. Serve a variety of breads this week (raisin, pita, sourdough, French, Italian, cornbread). Talk about how daily bread is needed by everyone.

## WEEKLY PLANNER

### On Sunday
Say a prayer of gratitude for the life-affirming bread of the Eucharist.

### On the Web
**www.blestarewe.com**

 Visit our Web site for the saint of the day and the reflection question of the week.

### Saint of the Week
 **Saint Francis Solano (1549–1610)**

Born in Spain, Francis Solano became a missionary to the New World in 1589. Fr. Francis ministered to Indians and Spanish colonists in Peru. He often played the lute and sang at Mass.

**Patron Saint of:** Chile and Peru
**Feast Day:** July 14

A Prayer for the Week

Saint Francis Solano prayed with music and song in different languages. O Lord, help us learn many ways to pray to you. Help us to always pray with an open heart. Amen.

# Take Home

FAMILY TIME

## ✝ Scripture Background

### Before the Time of Jesus

**Synagogues**   There was only one Temple, and it was in Jerusalem. There, Jews prayed and made sacrificial offerings. Synagogues, however, were spread throughout the Holy Land. Here, Jews assembled to pray, read Scripture, and hear teachings based on that Scripture. Prayers often focused on readings from the Pentateuch (the first five books of the Bible), and the prophets. Two central prayers in Judaism—the *Shema* and the *Amidah*—were included.

You can read Isaiah 61:1–2 to reflect on the Scripture Jesus later prayed in a synagogue.

## OUR CATHOLIC TRADITION in Symbols

**Blessed Palms**   In Jesus' time, people sometimes used objects as they prayed. Palm branches were used during prayers of praise. The waving branches symbolized victory. Jesus' followers held palm branches during his triumphant entry into Jerusalem before his passion and death.

Palms are blessed at the beginning of the Palm Sunday liturgy. The ashes crossed on our foreheads on Ash Wednesday come from burned palms. Some families place palms around a hanging crucifix or holy picture. Another tradition is braiding palms into crosses.

# 16 We Pray Like Jesus

Let us call to the LORD at all times.
Let us praise God both day and night.

Based on Psalm 34:2

## Share

Many people do things at the same time each day.

At 7:00 A.M., Betsy wakes up.
What time do you usually wake up?

_____

- - - - - - - - - - - - - - - - - - - - - - - - - - - - - -

_____

At 8:00 A.M., Willie gets on the bus.
What time do you go to school?

_____

- - - - - - - - - - - - - - - - - - - - - - - - - - - - - -

_____

Elm School

At 6:00 P.M., the Diaz family eats dinner.
What time does your family eat dinner?

_____

- - - - - - - - - - - - - - - - - - - - - - - - - - - - - -

_____

Talk about what time things happen on Saturday.

How did Jesus pray?

Tell what is different about Sunday.

# Hear & Believe

## ✝ Scripture The Prayer of Jesus

Jesus had prayed many times with his friends. One day, they asked Jesus to teach them to pray as he did. So, Jesus taught them this prayer.

Our Father
    who art in heaven,
      **hallowed** be thy name.
Thy kingdom come.
Thy will be done on earth,
    as it is in heaven.
Give us this day
    our daily bread,
and forgive us
    our **trespasses**,
    as we forgive those
    who trespass against us,
and lead us not
    into **temptation**,
    but deliver us from evil.
Amen.

Based on Luke 11:1; Matthew 6:9–13

184

## The Lord's Prayer

We call the prayer Jesus taught the **Lord's Prayer**. Jesus said that God's name is hallowed, or holy. We show respect for God's name. In this prayer, we remember that God is the Father of all people.

## Our Church Teaches

The Lord's Prayer is special because Jesus taught it to us. In it we ask forgiveness for our sins, our trespasses. We ask that we not have temptations. We do not want to do wrong. At every Mass we pray the Lord's Prayer. When we pray this prayer at Mass, we may hold out our open hands.

### We Believe

Jesus taught us to pray the Lord's Prayer. It is the prayer of Christians all over the world.

### Faith Words

**hallowed**
Hallowed is another word for "holy."

**trespasses**
Trespasses are sins or wrongs.

**temptation**
A temptation is wanting to do something that is wrong.

How do church members pray?

185

# Respond

## Praying Together

Mary and Joseph taught Jesus how to pray. They prayed at home and in the Temple. Our parents teach us how to pray. We pray together at home and in church. As church members we pray the Lord's Prayer together.

| The Lord's Prayer | What It Means |
|---|---|
| Our Father who art in heaven, hallowed be thy name. | We praise God the Father for being good and holy. |
| Thy kingdom come. Thy will be done on earth, as it is in heaven. | We pray God will bring about a time of perfect happiness and peace. We pray that everyone will obey God's laws. |
| Give us this day our daily bread, | We pray for our needs and the needs of others. |
| and forgive us our trespasses, as we forgive those who trespass against us, | We ask God to forgive our sins. We forgive people who have hurt us. |
| and lead us not into temptation, | We ask God to help us choose right instead of wrong. |
| but deliver us from evil. | We ask God to protect us from things that may harm us. |
| Amen. | We say "Yes, I believe. It is true." |

# Activities

Before eating, Catholics pray the Grace Before Meals. After eating, we pray the Grace After Meals.

**1.** Choose words from the box to complete these mealtime prayers. The pictures will help you.

> **gifts**   **receive**   **Christ**   **thanks**   **forever**

Bless us, O Lord, and these thy  _____, _____,

which we are about to  _____ from thy

bounty, through  _____ our Lord. Amen.

We give thee  _____ for all thy

 _____, almighty God, living and

reigning now and _____ Amen.

**2.** Learn these mealtime prayers by heart.

**What do we ask in the Lord's Prayer?**

# Prayer Celebration

## A Community Prayer

**Leader:** Jesus taught us the Lord's Prayer. This prayer to God the Father is a gift from Jesus to us.

**All:** **(Hold hands out, palms up.)**

**Reader 1:** We pray "Our Father." May all your people praise you.

**All:** **(Take right hand up to mouth.)**

**Reader 2:** We ask for daily bread. Please give us what we need this day.

**All:** **(Bow head, hands down.)**

**Reader 3:** We ask to be forgiven of our trespasses. Help us remember our promise to forgive others.

**All** **(Cross hands in front of face, palms out.)**

**Reader 4:** We ask to be delivered from evil. Protect us from harm.

**All:** **Amen.**

**(Share a handshake of peace.)**

# 16 Chapter Review

**A** **Complete** the sentences with words from the box.

| bread | holy | Mass |
|-------|------|------|

1. Hallowed means _____.

2. We pray the Lord's Prayer at every _____ _____.

3. We pray for our daily _____.

**B** **Circle** the correct answer.

1. Jesus taught the _____ to his followers.

   **Hail Mary**    **Lord's Prayer**    **Sign of the Cross**

2. Sins or wrongs we do on purpose are _____.

   **trespasses**    **deeds**    **grace**

3. Wanting to do something wrong is called _____.

   **blessed**    **temptation**    **hallowed**

4. We ask God to deliver us from _____.

   **evil**    **goodness**    **prayer**

5. Jesus taught us to call God our _____.

   **Son**    **Brother**    **Father**

# Faith in Action

**Catechists** The Holy Spirit calls men and women to be catechists. These are prayerful people who live their faith. Catechists teach religious education. Catechists try to help others grow in their faith. Families work with catechists to prepare their children for the sacraments.

## In Your Parish

**Activity** Color the shapes with a † blue. Color all other shapes yellow. **What do catechists help you grow in?**

## In Everyday Life

**Activity** Think of other people who teach you. Name these people and tell what you learn from them.

# We Go in Peace

Made stronger by the Eucharist, we work to be more like Christ in all we do. We can help others know about Jesus by the way we treat them.

*Blessed are the peacemakers,*
*for they will be called children of God.*
Matthew 5:9

Christ's first disciples may have walked this street in Jerusalem spreading a message of peace. At the end of Mass we also go in peace to serve all people.

# Alleluia

*Music by Fintan O'Carroll*

Al – le – lu – ia, al – le – lu – ia!

Al – le – lu – ia, al – le – lu – ia!

© 1985, GIA Publications, Inc.

**FAMILY TIME**

# God Gives Us the Holy Spirit

God gives us the Holy Spirit to guide us in our daily lives. The children will come to understand that the Holy Spirit is our helper, guide, and teacher. They will think about and appreciate the spiritual gifts that Paul writes about in the Scripture passage.

## ACTIVITY

**Matching Gifts** Have a family gift night! Each person can give a small present to one other family member. Choose names beforehand so that everyone gets a present. The present should represent a talent the person has. For example, if someone draws well, the gift might be a sketch pad.

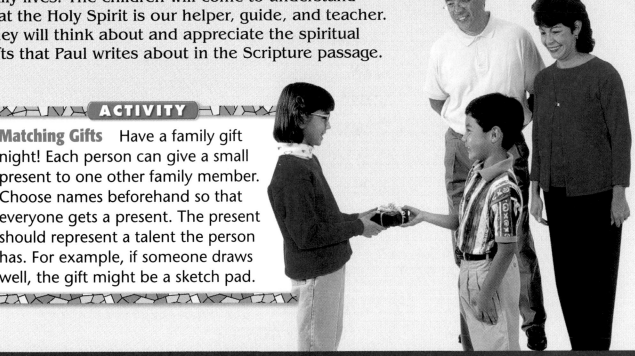

## WEEKLY PLANNER

### On Sunday

Pray for the people who, in the name of the congregation, bring up the gifts in the offertory procession.

### On the Web

**www.blestarewe.com**

Visit our Web site for the saint of the day and the reflection question of the week.

### Saint of the Week

 **Saint Catherine of Siena** (1347–1380)

Catherine was the youngest of twenty-five children in her family. She became a Dominican sister. God gave Saint Catherine the gift of wisdom which she used to give advice and guidance to others.

**Patron Saint of:** firefighters, nurses, and sick people
**Feast Day:** April 29

### A Prayer for the Week

Holy Spirit, thank you for the gifts of wisdom and knowledge. May we use them as Saint Catherine of Siena did to help others. May we always be faithful followers of Jesus. Amen.

# Take Home

FAMILY TIME

## ✝ Scripture Background

### In the Time of the Early Church

**Corinth**   Corinth was a bustling seaport city in Greece. As such, it attracted people of various religions. Paul cherished the Christian community in Corinth, even though factions within the community caused him much frustration. In his first letter, Paul reminds the Corinthians of Jesus' message — the need for correct behavior in worship, a call for peaceful coexistence, and the power of true Christian love.

You can read of Paul's concerns for his people in 1 Corinthians 12.

# OUR CATHOLIC TRADITION in Architecture

**Hagia Sofia**   The Hagia Sofia, Greek for "holy wisdom," was built in the sixth century by the emperor Justinian I in Constantinople, now Istanbul, Turkey. The cathedral was named for the gift of the Holy Spirit and remains one of the finest examples of Byzantine architecture.

After the Turks conquered Constantinople in the fifteenth century, the Hagia Sophia became a mosque, or Islamic house of worship. Its mosaics and Christian symbols were covered with plaster. The Hagia Sofia stayed that way until the twentieth century, when it became a museum and some of its original mosaics were uncovered.

# 17 God Gives Us the Holy Spirit

**LET US PRAY** God has sent the Holy Spirit into our hearts.

Based on Galatians 4:6

## Share

All people have special gifts. These gifts are part of who we are. We can use these gifts to help others.

Some people are smart. They can help others learn.

Some people are funny. They can cheer up people who are sad.

Some people are kind and helpful. They can make life easier for others.

What is one special gift you have?

_____

I can _____.

What are spiritual gifts?

How can you use this gift to help others?

# Hear & Believe

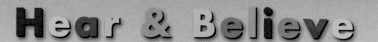

## ✝ Scripture  The Special Gifts

Some of Paul's friends lived in the city of Corinth. They asked Paul about the best way to serve God and their community. Paul wrote this letter to them.

Dear Friends,

God loves you very much. God sends you the Holy Spirit. The Holy Spirit helps you to live as good followers of Jesus.

The Holy Spirit helps by giving special gifts to each person. They are called **spiritual gifts**. Some of these gifts are wisdom, healing, knowledge, and faith. The Holy Spirit may give one person the gift of wisdom. He may give another person the gift of healing. To someone else, he may give knowledge or faith.

Show your love for God by sharing your gifts with each other. The church community needs each person's gifts!

Peace and love,
Paul

Based on 1 Corinthians 12:4–11

## Gifts to Share

Paul's letter says that the Holy Spirit gives each of us spiritual gifts. Some gifts are knowledge, wisdom, healing, and faith. We show our love for God by using our gifts to help others.

## Our Church Teaches

We receive the Holy Spirit in the sacraments. The Holy Spirit is our helper, guide, and teacher. He helps us share our gifts with other people and with the Church. The Holy Spirit guides us in our daily lives.

### We Believe

The Holy Spirit gives us spiritual gifts to share with others. These gifts help us follow Jesus.

### Faith Words

**spiritual gifts** The Holy Spirit gives us spiritual gifts. Some of these gifts are knowledge, wisdom, healing, and faith.

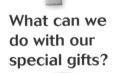

What can we do with our special gifts?

# Respond

## Using Our Gifts

Religion class had just started. Mrs. Foy asked, "How do you use your spiritual gifts to help others?"

Gino said, "I help my little sister learn to count. That's how I use my gift of knowledge."

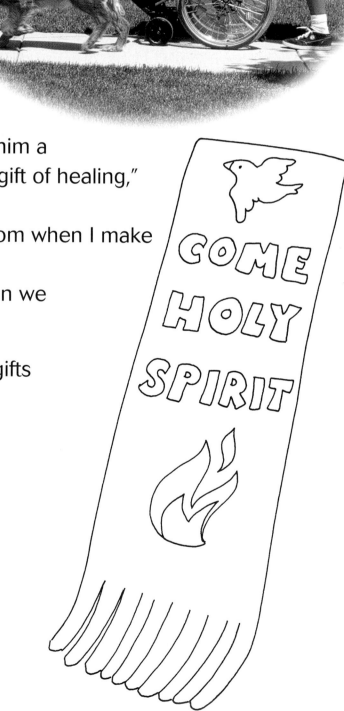

"Sometimes Dad gets hot and tired from working outdoors. I bring him a nice cold drink. That's how I use my gift of healing," added Tara.

Kathy said, "I use the gift of wisdom when I make good choices."

"All of us use the gift of faith when we trust in God," said Jake.

? How do you use your spiritual gifts to help others?

## Activities

1. Sometimes we use symbols to stand for the Holy Spirit. Some symbols are a white dove, wind, flames, and rays of light. Color the symbols and the words in the banner.

COME HOLY SPIRIT

**2.** God wants us to open our hearts to the Holy Spirit. God wants us to use the gifts we have been given.

Put a ✓ under **Yes** if the person is using his or her gifts. Put a ✓ under **No** if the person is not using his or her gifts.

|  | Yes | No |
|---|---|---|
| **a.** Janet receives a letter from Grandma. She does not answer it. | ☐ | ☐ |
| **b.** Carlos shares his popcorn with Max and Ricardo. | ☐ | ☐ |
| **c.** Mike can read. He does not want to help his little sister learn to read. | ☐ | ☐ |
| **d.** Debra can draw beautiful pictures. She draws one for Aunt Sue. | ☐ | ☐ |
| **e.** Susan likes to sing. She sings in the children's choir at Mass. | ☐ | ☐ |
| **f.** Robert plays the piano very well, but he will not play for others. | ☐ | ☐ |
| **g.** Tanya tells bedtime stories to her little sister. | ☐ | ☐ |

**How can we celebrate our spiritual gifts?**

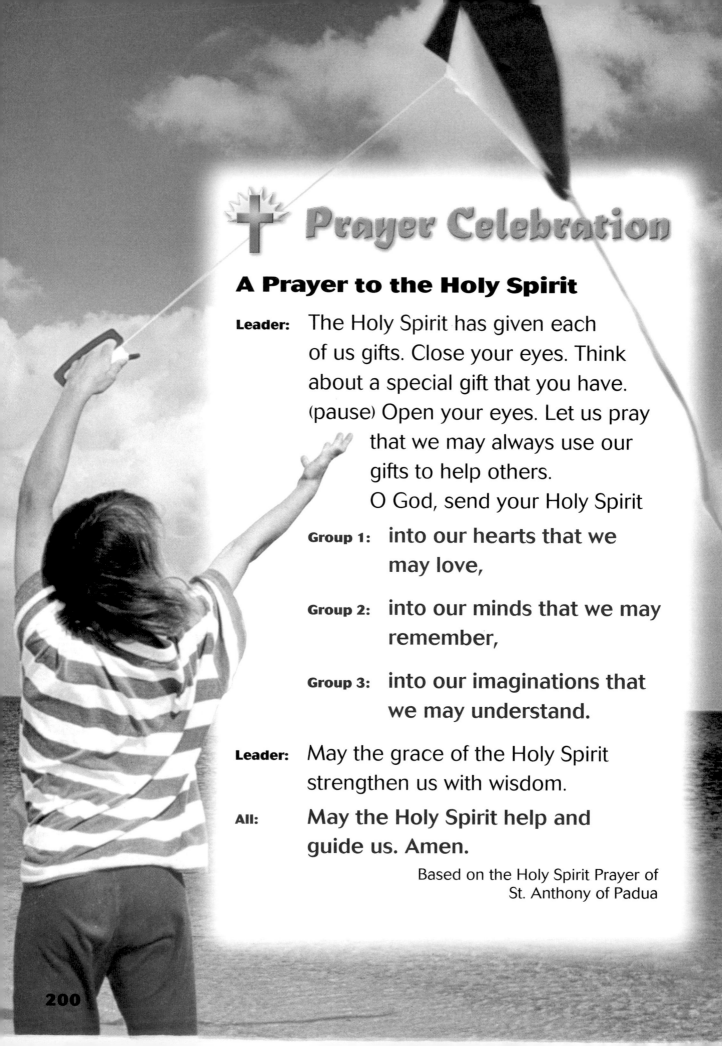

## ✝ Prayer Celebration

### A Prayer to the Holy Spirit

**Leader:** The Holy Spirit has given each of us gifts. Close your eyes. Think about a special gift that you have. (pause) Open your eyes. Let us pray that we may always use our gifts to help others.
O God, send your Holy Spirit

**Group 1:** into our hearts that we may love,

**Group 2:** into our minds that we may remember,

**Group 3:** into our imaginations that we may understand.

**Leader:** May the grace of the Holy Spirit strengthen us with wisdom.

**All:** May the Holy Spirit help and guide us. Amen.

Based on the Holy Spirit Prayer of
St. Anthony of Padua

**A** **Write** about what the Holy Spirit wants us to do with our spiritual gifts.

_____

- - - - - - - - - - - - - - - - - - - - - - - - - - - - - - -

_____

_____

- - - - - - - - - - - - - - - - - - - - - - - - - - - - - - -

_____

**B** **Circle** the words that best complete the sentences.

1. The church community needs the _____ of each person.
   **belongings**       **gifts**       **pictures**

2. The Holy Spirit is our helper, guide, and _____.
   **parent**       **priest**       **teacher**

3. God wants us to open our _____ to the Holy Spirit.
   **books**       **desks**       **hearts**

4. Knowledge, wisdom, and faith are _____ gifts from the Holy Spirit.
   **expensive**       **song**       **spiritual**

5. Spiritual gifts help us to follow _____.
   **angels**       **Jesus**       **strangers**

## Faith in Action

**Pastoral Assistants**  Pastoral assistants bring together the work of all parish ministers. They might plan liturgy or visit the sick. They help people in the parish use their spiritual gifts. Pastoral assistants work with priests, deacons, and other leaders in the parish.

**In Your Parish**

**Activity**  Think about all the people you see who lead activities in your parish. What gift from the Holy Spirit might you have to serve your parish?

**In Everyday Life**

**Activity**  The sentences below tell about leaders and the people they lead. Unscramble the words.

- At school a principal leads CAERHETS _____.

- Coaches lead players on a AMTE _____.

- In a restaurant, a manager leads OFDO _____ servers.

# Take Home

FAMILY TIME

# We Celebrate Peace and Service

The children will learn that we greet each other at Mass by offering those around us a Sign of Peace. This sign reminds us that Jesus wants us to get along with everyone and to serve one another.

**ACTIVITY**

**Greetings** Play a game with your child in which you take turns making different gestures to say Hello, such as waving. See how many turns you can take without repeating the same gesture.

## WEEKLY PLANNER

### On Sunday
Remind each other to think about making peace in the family as you share the Sign of Peace at Mass.

### On the Web

**www.blestarewe.com**
Visit our Web site for the saint of the day and the reflection question of the week.

### Saint of the Week

 **Saint Anthony of Padua** (1195–1231)

Anthony of Padua preached and taught men who were training to be priests. He also taught people who felt lost and confused. He was a Franciscan friar. Saint Anthony died when he was only thirty-six.

**Patron Saint of:** seekers of lost articles, animals
**Feast Day:** June 13

A Prayer for the Week

O God, may we always be willing to serve you and your people. Help us to see your presence in everyone we meet. May we follow the example of Saint Anthony of Padua. Amen.

# Take Home

FAMILY TIME

## ✝ Scripture Background

### In the Time of the Early Church

**Agape**   The Greek word *agape* means love. In the New Testament, it designates the unmerited love God shows to humankind by sending Jesus as suffering redeemer. It is connected to a fellowship meal following the celebration of Eucharist. When applied to human love, *agape* means selfless and self-giving love.

You can read about this form of true Christian love that Paul speaks of in 1 Corinthians 13.

# OUR CATHOLIC TRADITION in Religious Life

**Bl. Jeanne Jugan**   Blessed Jeanne Jugan, Marie of the Cross (1792–1879), grew up as a poor French girl. From her youth she felt that she was called to do something special. In 1837, with another woman and a teenage orphan girl, she formed a community of prayer and good works. From that small beginning, she established an order called the Little Sisters of the Poor, whose mission is to care for the needy elderly. In addition to the vows of poverty, chastity, and obedience, this group takes a vow of hospitality. On October 3, 1982, Jeanne Jugan was beatified by Pope John Paul II. Today, there are Little Sisters of the Poor in thirty countries, on five continents.

# 18 We Celebrate Peace and Service

 Grace and peace to you from God our Father and the Lord Jesus Christ.

Based on 2 Corinthians 1:2

## Share

We greet other people with words or with actions.

The people in the pictures want to say "Hello."
Each of them wants to say it in a different way.
Write a different greeting below for each person.

How do we greet each other at Mass?

# Hear & Believe

## Worship The Sign of Peace

At each Eucharist, we offer those around us a Sign of Peace. Peace is a sign that the Holy Spirit is with us. This sign reminds us that Jesus wants us to get along with everyone. It reminds us that we are to serve one another each day.

We share the Sign of Peace in this way:

**Priest:** Lord Jesus Christ, you said to your apostles:
I leave you peace, my peace I give you.
Look not on our sins, but on the faith of your Church,
and grant us the peace and unity of your kingdom
where you live for ever and ever.

**All:** Amen.

**Priest:** The peace of the Lord be with you always.

**All:** And also with you.

**Priest:** Let us offer each other the sign of peace.

The Order of Mass

## We Take Part and Serve

The Sign of Peace reminds us that Jesus wants us to love one another. Jesus wants us to have peace. The Sign of Peace calls the whole church community to serve one another. It reminds us to take part in parish activities.

## Our Church Teaches

Holy Orders and Matrimony are Sacraments at the Service of Communion. In **Holy Orders**, men become deacons, priests, or bishops. They help teach and serve the People of God.

In **Matrimony** a man and woman promise to love and serve each other and their children. They promise to be faithful to each other for their whole lives. Married people also share in the work of the parish.

### We Believe

Holy Orders and Matrimony are Sacraments at the Service of Communion.

### Faith Words

**Holy Orders**
Holy Orders is a sacrament in which bishops, priests, and deacons are ordained to special service.

**Matrimony**
Matrimony is a sacrament in which a man and woman promise to be faithful to each other for their whole lives.

How can we celebrate our call to service?

# Respond
## Choosing to Serve

Joseph Ratzinger was born in a tiny village in Germany in 1927. When he was five years old he met a cardinal for the first time. Joseph was part of a group of children who presented the visiting cardinal with flowers. After that visit he decided to become a cardinal himself. Before then he had wanted to be a bricklayer.

Joseph did not like sports but enjoyed walks in the mountains. He still enjoys music and plays the piano.

Joseph and his older brother, George, studied for the priesthood together. In 1951 both brothers celebrated the Sacrament of Holy Orders. In 1977 Pope Paul VI named Joseph archbishop and then cardinal. He was living his childhood dream!

Cardinal Ratzinger later became an advisor to Pope John Paul II. He served as advisor until the pope's death. The Church needed a new pope. On April 19, 2005 other cardinals chose Cardinal Ratzinger to serve. He took the name Pope Benedict XVI. He said, "I am a humble servant in God's vineyard."

# Activities

**1.** Color each space that has a †. Write the hidden message on the line below the picture. Then color the picture.

_____

\- \- \- \- \- \- \- \- \- \- \- \- \- \- \- \- \- \- \- \- \- \-

_____.

**2.** Complete these sentences.

A bride and groom celebrate the Sacrament of

_____

\- \- \- \- \- \- \- \- \- \- \- \- \- \- \- \- \- \- \- \- \- \-

_____.

When a man becomes a priest, he receives

_____

\- \- \- \- \- \- \- \- \- \- \- \- \- \- \- \- \- \- \- \- \- \-

_____

How can we celebrate people who serve oth

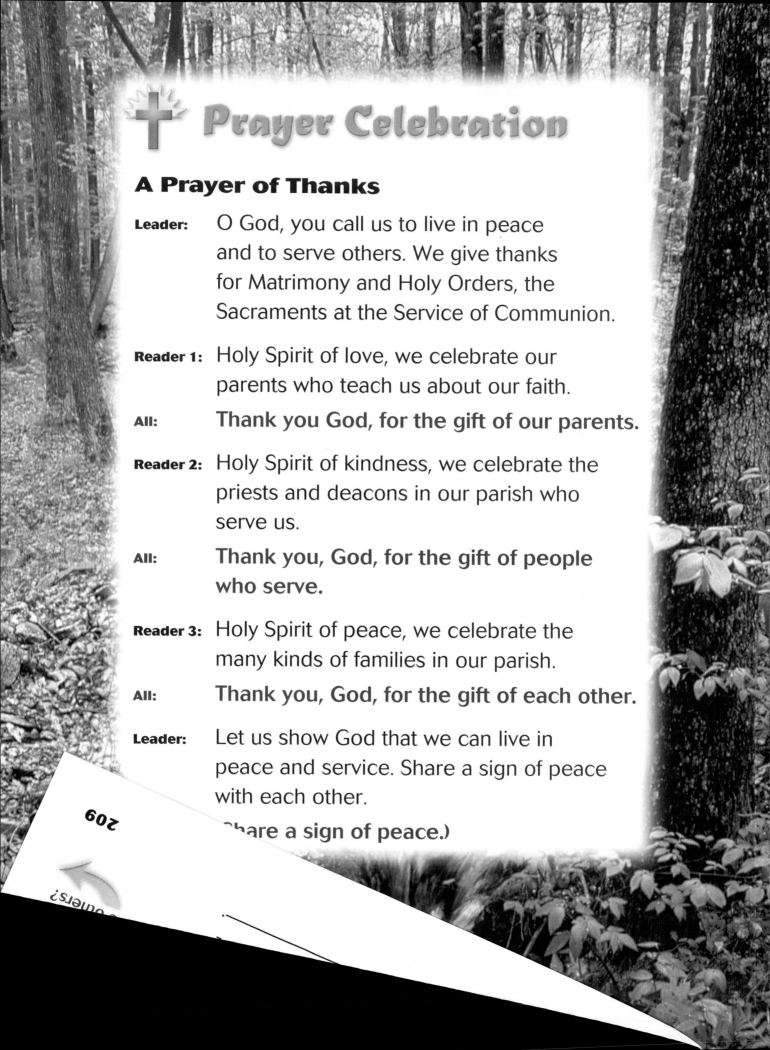

# Prayer Celebration

## A Prayer of Thanks

**Leader:** O God, you call us to live in peace and to serve others. We give thanks for Matrimony and Holy Orders, the Sacraments at the Service of Communion.

**Reader 1:** Holy Spirit of love, we celebrate our parents who teach us about our faith.

**All:** **Thank you God, for the gift of our parents.**

**Reader 2:** Holy Spirit of kindness, we celebrate the priests and deacons in our parish who serve us.

**All:** **Thank you, God, for the gift of people who serve.**

**Reader 3:** Holy Spirit of peace, we celebrate the many kinds of families in our parish.

**All:** **Thank you, God, for the gift of each other.**

**Leader:** Let us show God that we can live in peace and service. Share a sign of peace with each other.

hare a sign of peace.)

# 18 Chapter Review

**A** **Draw** a line to connect the parts of each sentence.

1. At Mass we offer each other the _____.

   • • **Sign of Peace**

2. Peace is a sign that the _____ is with us.

   • • **Holy Spirit**

3. Deacons, priests, and bishops receive the Sacrament of _____.

   • • **get along**

4. In Matrimony a man and woman promise to be faithful to _____.

   • • **Holy Orders**

5. The Sign of Peace reminds us that Jesus wants us to _____ with everyone.

   • • **one another**

**B** **Complete** the sentences with words from the box.

1. A baptized bride and groom receive

   _____

   the Sacrament of _____.

2. Deacons, priests, and bishops teach

   _____

   and serve the _____ of God.

3. Married people serve the Church by sharing in

   _____

   the _____ of their parish.

| People |
| Matrimony |
| work |

# Faith in Action

**Ushers**   Jesus calls us to serve each other. We do this in many ways. At church, some people serve as ushers. They help people find seats. They collect money offerings. Ushers guide people going to Communion. They help people who become sick or hurt.

## In Everyday Life

**Activity**   Think about how people in your family serve each other. Name two ways you serve family members. Name two ways family members serve you.

## In Your Parish

**Activity**   Color the boxes yellow that show service at church. Color green the ones that are not service. Write your own idea of service in the empty box. Color it yellow.

opening a door for just yourself

helping carry groceries

making thank-you cards

putting away song books

leaving paper in pew

# Take Home

FAMILY TIME

# We Work for Peace and Justice

The saying "If you want peace, work for justice" sums up the Christian belief in the interconnectedness of the two. We are called to treat others fairly and with respect. In Chapter 19 children will consider the concepts of peace and justice and identify actions they can take to promote these concepts. The children will realize that Jesus taught us to treat others fairly and respectfully.

## ACTIVITY

**Certificate of Fairness** With your child, make a simple certificate with construction paper and bright-colored decorations. Help your child write the words *Fairness Counts* at the top. List words associated with fairness, such as *sharing, helping,* and *giving.* Each time your child acts fairly this week, give her or him a sticker to add to the certificate.

## WEEKLY PLANNER

### On Sunday
Other than in the Sign of Peace, when is peace mentioned in the liturgy? Listen for other mentions of peace.

### On the Web
**www.blestarewe.com**

Visit our Web site for the saint of the day and the reflection question of the week.

### Saint of the Week

**Saint Catherine of Alexandria** (?–305)

Catherine of Alexandria lived in Africa. She was an intelligent woman who opposed evil and lived a life of truth and justice. After challenging the pagan emperor she was martyred for her faith.

**Patron Saint of:** craftspeople, scholars, students
**Feast Day:** November 25

### A Prayer for the Week

Lord, you call upon us to speak up for what is true and just. May we have the courage to work for peace and justice as did Saint Catherine of Alexandria. Amen.

# Getting ready for Chapter 19

# Take Home

FAMILY TIME

## ✝ Scripture Background

### In the Time of the Early Church

**First Christian Community** Peter set up the first Christian community in Jerusalem. Here Christians tried to adhere to the teachings of the Apostles, and center their religious life in the Eucharistic liturgy. Through a system of fair distribution, the wealthy sold their possessions for the needs of the poor. At the time, followers of Jesus continued the practice of Temple worship as Jews.

You can read of the efforts of early Christians in Acts 2:42–47, 4:32–37.

## OUR CATHOLIC TRADITION in Volunteerism

**Catholic Network of Volunteer Service** In 1963, the non-profit organization of Catholic Network of Volunteer Service (CNVS) was formed. Its goal is to help women and men use their gifts by volunteering service to others. Special programs help connect volunteers with volunteer opportunities. CNVS supports community-based programs such as Americorps, which is the domestic Peace Corps. This volunteer program encourages youth to help other youth with issues involving illiteracy, poverty, crime, homelessness, and environmental problems.

# 19 We Work for Peace and Justice

LET US PRAY

Happy are those who are fair with others.
Happy are those who make peace.

Based on Matthew 5:6, 9

# Share

Life is not always fair. Some people are rich, while others are poor. Some people are healthy, while others are sick.

Look at the pictures. Use a ✔ to mark each one **fair** or **unfair**.

**She shares.**

☐ fair ☐ unfair

**He steals.**

☐ fair ☐ unfair

**She helps.**

☐ fair ☐ unfair

**He gives.**

☐ fair ☐ unfair

**She peeks.**

☐ fair ☐ unfair

How does Jesus want us to act?

# Hear & Believe

## ✝ Scripture  The First Followers of Jesus

The first followers of Jesus tried to treat everyone fairly. If life was not fair, they tried to help make it better. Here is how the early Christians treated one another.

The Christians were all of one heart and
  one mind.
They tried to make peace and they tried
  to be kind.
They shared what they had, both the rich
  and the poor,
So no one went hungry or wanted for more.
Those who had extra would sell what they had.
They took care of those who were sick or were sad.
If someone were needy, other Christians came.
They brought food or money in Christ Jesus' name.

Based on Acts 4:32–35

## What Jesus Taught

Jesus taught us to live in **peace**. When there is fighting, Christians try to make peace. Jesus also taught us to treat everyone fairly, with **justice**. We comfort people who need extra help. We share with people who have less.

## Our Church Teaches

We are to treat people the way we want to be treated. We grow in holiness when we make peace and treat others fairly. The Holy Spirit helps us to live as faithful members of our Church.

### We Believe

God's Spirit helps us do what is right. Christians believe that all people deserve to be treated with justice.

### Faith Words

**peace**
Peace means getting along with others.

**justice**
Justice means to treat people fairly.

How can we make peace and act with justice?

# Respond
## Christian Peacemakers

Peacemakers try to make peace when there is fighting and trouble. They try to bring justice to people who need it. Here are some Christians who are peacemakers.

Doctor Johnson works with Operation Smile. He helps children in need. He fixes their faces so they can smile again.

A soldier helps keep peace in another country. He does not want fighting to start again.

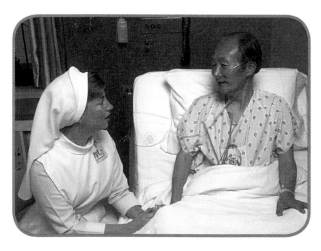

Sister Carole Martin helps people who are sick or dying. She shows them that God has not forgotten them.

Mrs. Brown works in a shelter for women and children. She protects them from people who want to hurt them.

# Activity

Get ready for the prayer celebration. Learn to sign the words "Blessed are the peacemakers, for they will be called children of God" (Matthew 5:9).

**Blessed**       **peacemakers,**

**they**      **will be**      **called**

**children**      **God**

How can we celebrate God's gifts of peace and justice?

219

# Prayer Celebration

## A Signing Prayer

**Leader:** O God, we ask you to bless those who work for peace and justice. We pray for all people who try to stop wars and make peace.

**All:** (*Sign:* Blessed are the peacemakers.)

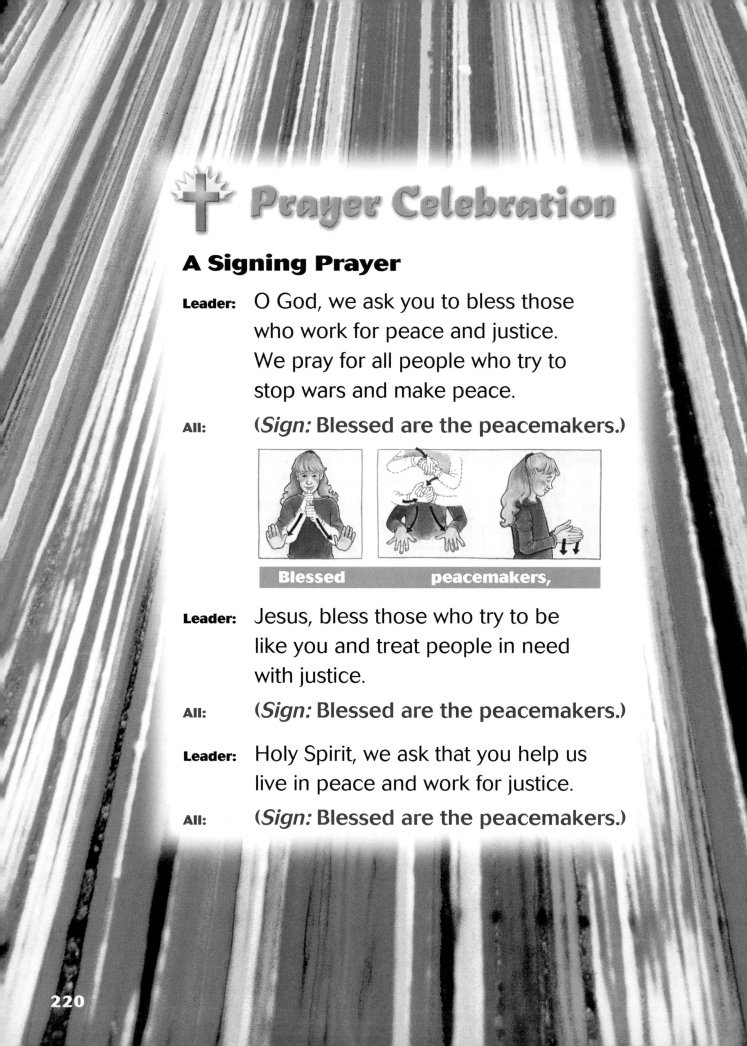

Blessed          peacemakers,

**Leader:** Jesus, bless those who try to be like you and treat people in need with justice.

**All:** (*Sign:* Blessed are the peacemakers.)

**Leader:** Holy Spirit, we ask that you help us live in peace and work for justice.

**All:** (*Sign:* Blessed are the peacemakers.)

**A** **Write or draw** one way to get along with someone.

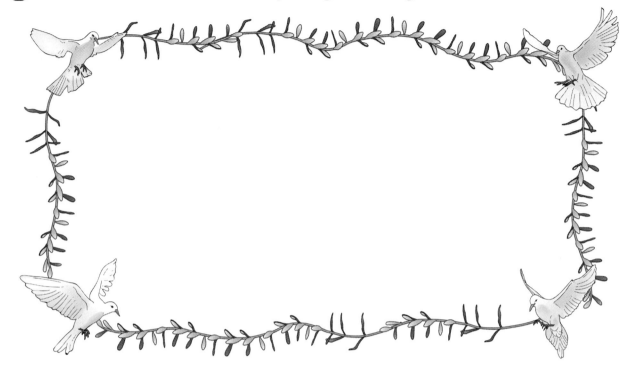

**B** **Circle** the words that best complete the sentences.

**1.** Christians try to make _____.
money        peace        food

**2.** _____ means getting along with others.
Peace        Justice        Healthy

**3.** _____ is fair treatment for everyone.
Peace        Justice        Stealing

**4.** We grow in _____ when we make peace.
age        fear        holiness

**5.** God's Spirit helps us do what is _____.
popular        right        wrong

# Faith in Action

**Parish Secretary**   All parishes need someone to welcome visitors and help parish members. Parish secretaries greet visitors, answer phones, and open mail. They assist their pastor. They also support people in different parish ministries. Some prepare the weekly bulletin. A parish secretary gets to meet many people.

**In Your Parish**

**Activity**   Think about work that people do at church. How can you thank them for their work?

**In Everyday Life**

**Activity**   How do these workers help others? Match the letter for each worker with that worker's help.

**a.** crossing guard ☐ Helps us be healthy.

**b.** bus driver ☐ Helps us learn new things.

**c.** doctor ☐ Brings us letters.

**d.** mail carrier ☐ Helps us cross streets safely.

**e.** teacher ☐ Gets us places we want to go.

# Take Home

FAMILY TIME

## We Go Forth in the Holy Spirit

Chapter 20 will highlight the virtue of peace and the beauty of blessings. Children will realize that blessings are signs of God's love, that we bless God when we praise and thank him, and that we can pray to God to bless others. They will recognize that the Holy Spirit guides us when we pray, and they will compose prayers of blessings.

### ACTIVITY

**Bless This Mess** Some families have in their homes a sign that bears the motto "Bless This Mess." It invites God to be part of the family's life even though the house may not be perfectly neat and clean. With your child, make a sign that asks for God's blessing on the activities of your family.

## WEEKLY PLANNER

### On Sunday

At the end of Mass when the priest says, "Go in peace to love and serve the Lord," think of one way to do that.

### On the Web

**www.blestarewe.com**

 Visit our Web site for the saint of the day and the reflection question of the week.

### Saint of the Week

 **Saint Rose Philippine Duchesne** (1769–1852)

Rose Philippine Duchesne joined the Society of the Sacred Heart in France. Mother Duchesne came to the United States to open schools for children of pioneers and Native American people.

**Patron Saint of:** Native Americans

**Feast Day:** November 18

 A Prayer for the Week

O God, thank you for the many blessing you give us. May we follow the example of Saint Rose Philippine Duchesne and be willing to bless others. Amen.

# Take Home

FAMILY TIME

## ✝ Scripture Background

### Before the Time of Jesus

**Blessings**   The first Old Testament blessing is described in Genesis 1:28. After creating humankind, God says, "Be fertile and multiply." This is also called a "benediction," which means "saying good things." Fertility blessings and other common blessings involve health, longevity, the satisfying of needs, and a generally happy life. Jesus would carry on the ritual of blessings during his earthly life.

You can read about the first blessing in Genesis 1:24–31.

## OUR CATHOLIC TRADITION in Architecture

### Church of the Beatitudes

In the place where Jesus spoke the Beatitudes to his followers, there is a church that is named after them. The Church of the Beatitudes is located along the northern shore of the Sea of Galilee on the mount near Capernaum, home to five of Jesus' Twelve Apostles. Built in 1937, the church is octagonal to represent the eight Beatitudes that Matthew describes in his Gospel (Matthew 5:3–10). Inscribed on each window are the beginning words of one of the Beatitudes. A dome of gold mosaic covers the altar and rests on top of the building. Surrounding the outside of the church are columned cloisters. These provide a panoramic view of the Sea of Galilee.

# 20 We Go Forth in the Holy Spirit

May God help us be strong in our faith.
May God bless us with peace.

Based on Psalm 29:11

## Share

God's gifts are all around us. These gifts make us happy. We receive God's gifts through our five senses. Think about the good things that have happened to you this year. Write about them here.

 Something beautiful I saw

_____

- - - - - - - - - - - - - - - - - - - - - - - - - - -

_____

Something wonderful I heard

_____

- - - - - - - - - - - - - - - - - - - - - - - - - - -

_____

Something nice I smelled

_____

- - - - - - - - - - - - - - - - - - - - - - - - - - -

_____

Something good I tasted

_____

- - - - - - - - - - - - - - - - - - - - - - - - - - -

_____

Something soft I touched

_____

- - - - - - - - - - - - - - - - - - - - - - - - - - -

_____

How can we praise God and bless other people?

# Hear & Believe

## ✝ Scripture  God's Grace and Blessing

God spoke to Moses one day. God said, "Moses, speak to your brother Aaron and his sons. Tell them how to **bless** others." "All right," Moses answered. Then Moses told Aaron and his sons, "God wants you to bless people. Pray for them and say, 'May God bless you and keep you safe!

May God smile upon you.

May God look upon you kindly.

May God always give you peace.'"

Based on Numbers 6:22–26

## Signs of God's Love

A **blessing** is a sign of God's love for us. God told Moses how to give blessings to other people. The Holy Spirit helps us offer prayers of blessing to God. We bless God when we give praise and thanks for his many gifts.

## Our Church Teaches

When we bless God, we give him thanks and praise. We ask God to bless others. We ask that he fill others with love and peace. We ask God to bless us. And, we ask for God's help through the Holy Spirit.

### Faith Words

**bless**
To bless means to ask for God's good will toward someone.

**blessing**
A blessing asks for God's gifts for others or for ourselves.

How can we share our blessings with others?

# Respond

## We Love and Serve

Each Mass ends with a blessing. The priest asks God to bless us. He reminds us to carry on the work of Jesus. We do this by helping, caring for, and serving others.

**Priest:** May almighty God bless you, the Father, and the Son, and the Holy Spirit.

**All:** Amen.

**Priest:** Go in peace to love and serve the Lord.

**All:** Thanks be to God.

The Order of Mass

## WAYS TO LOVE AND SERVE OTHERS

We can be kind and patient.

We can cheerfully do chores and homework.

We can try to be helpful.

We can care for plants and animals.

We can share.

We can take part in parish activities.

We can ask God to bless others.

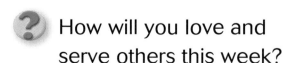 How will you love and serve others this week?

228

# Activities

**1.** Read the blessing prayer from God again.
Complete each sentence. Use the missing words
to complete the puzzle.

> May God (3 down) you and keep you (5 across)!
> May God (6 across) upon you.
> May God look upon you (4 across).
> May God always (1 down) you (2 down).

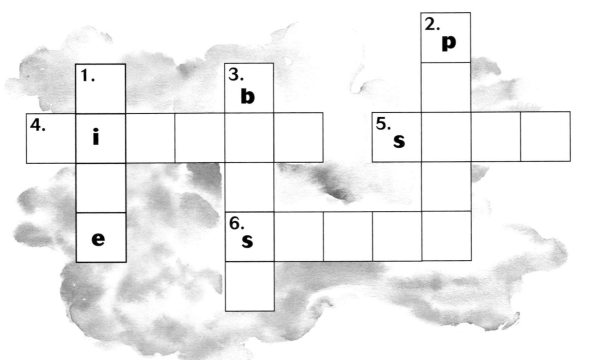

**2.** Write your own prayer of blessing.

_____

- - - - - - - - - - - - - - - - - - - - - -

May God bless you and _____

_____

- - - - - - - - - - - - - - - - - - - - - - - - - -

_____ .

How can we
celebrate
God's
blessings?

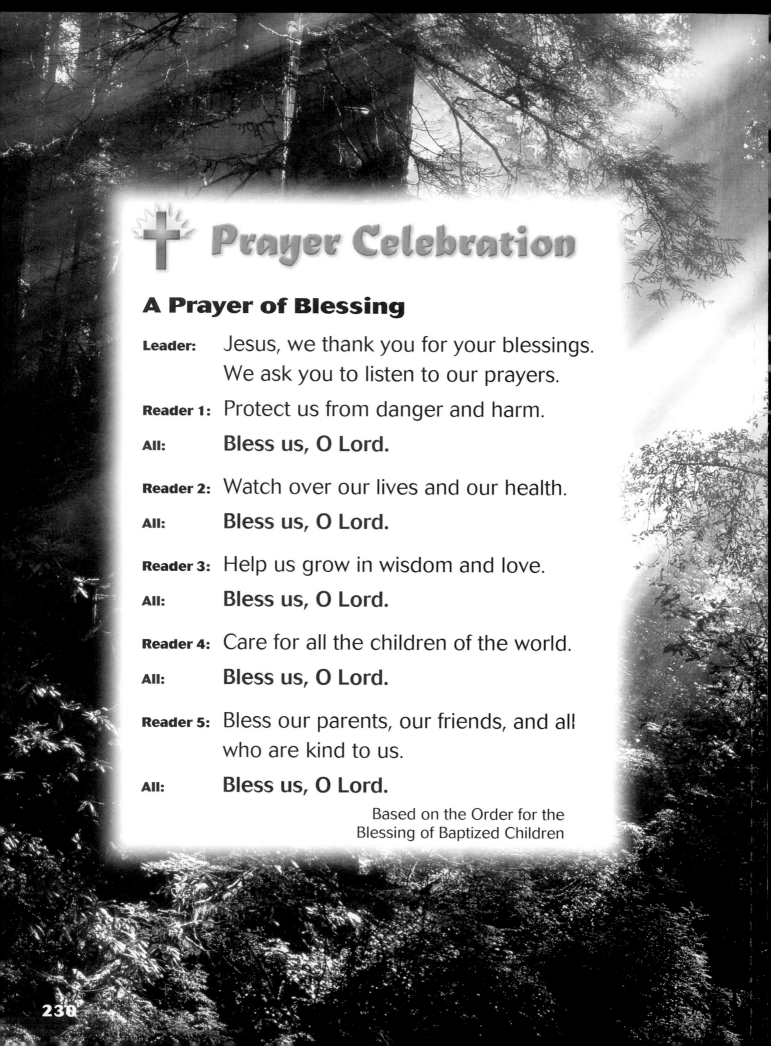

# ✝ Prayer Celebration

## A Prayer of Blessing

**Leader:** Jesus, we thank you for your blessings. We ask you to listen to our prayers.

**Reader 1:** Protect us from danger and harm.

**All:** **Bless us, O Lord.**

**Reader 2:** Watch over our lives and our health.

**All:** **Bless us, O Lord.**

**Reader 3:** Help us grow in wisdom and love.

**All:** **Bless us, O Lord.**

**Reader 4:** Care for all the children of the world.

**All:** **Bless us, O Lord.**

**Reader 5:** Bless our parents, our friends, and all who are kind to us.

**All:** **Bless us, O Lord.**

Based on the Order for the
Blessing of Baptized Children

# 20 Chapter Review

**A** **Circle** the best answer.

1. Which word means "to ask for God's good will"?
   bless          generous       grace

2. What did God tell Moses to give to other people?
   gifts          maps       blessings

3. To whom does God give blessings?
   priests        pope       everyone

4. What is a blessing a sign of?
   hate          love       summer

5. Who is it that the Holy Spirit helps us give prayers of blessing to?
   Adam         God       Moses

**B** **Write** the letter on each line for the word that best fits.

1. Moses told Aaron to say, "May God always give you _____."

2. When we ask God to bless others, we ask him to fill them with _____ and peace.

3. When we bless God, we give thanks and _____ to God.

4. We ask for God's _____ through the Holy Spirit.

> A love
>
> B help
>
> C peace
>
> D praise

# Faith in Action

**Sharing with Others**  Children in Tyler's parish wanted to help others. Their teacher told them about a parish with many needs. The boys and girls there had no money to buy books. Tyler and his friends decided to share their books. Tyler's friends hoped the children in the other parish would enjoy these books.

## In Your Parish

**Activity**  Think about ways your parish helps people in need. Maybe members collect food and money. What do you think would be another way to help others?

## In Everyday Life

**Activity**  Maybe there are books or other things you could share. Do you have good clothes that don't fit anymore? Do you have toys, or games that you don't use?

List things that you could share with children in need.

# FEASTS AND SEASONS

# The Church Year

Catholics celebrate seasons of the church year. Each Sunday begins a special week. There are five seasons. Each has its own symbols and colors.

**Holy Week** includes Palm Sunday, Holy Thursday, Good Friday, and Easter. We think about Jesus sharing a meal with his Apostles, his dying on a cross, and rising to new life.

**HOLY WEEK**

Our church year begins with **Advent**. For four weeks we prepare to celebrate the birth of Jesus.

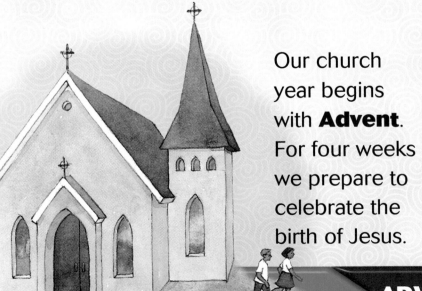

**ADVENT**

*The church year begins.*

## ORDINARY TIME

In **Ordinary Time** we learn about the life of Jesus. This season has two parts—between the seasons of Christmas and Lent, and between those of Easter and Advent.

**Easter** celebrates Jesus' Resurrection. It is a season of joy. It lasts fifty days until Pentecost. Then we celebrate the coming of the Holy Spirit.

**EASTER**

The season of **Lent** lasts forty days. It begins with Ash Wednesday. We prepare for Easter through prayer and spiritual works.

**LENT** **ORDINARY TIME**

At **Christmas** we celebrate the birthday of Jesus. It is a season of gift-giving and joy.

**CHRISTMAS**

**Feasts and Seasons** 235

# Sundays and Feast Days

Sunday is our greatest holy day. Sundays are important days to celebrate our Catholic faith.

We come together at Mass to celebrate Jesus' Resurrection. We celebrate Eucharist with our parish community. It is good to come together in community.

Sunday is a day to be happy, to rest and enjoy being with our families.

We celebrate many feast days during the church year. They honor Jesus, Mary, and the saints. These feast days help us grow in our faith.

# Feast of All Saints

 People will know that you are my friends,
if you love one another.

Based on John 13:35

## What's in a Name?

Every person has a name that is special to him or
her. Our names tell some interesting things about us.

**Jovito**

## Activity

What is your first name?

**GISELA**

_____

- - - - - - - - - - - - - - - - - - - - - - - - - - - - - - -

_____

Why did your parents give you that name?

**Roger**

Check (✓) the reasons below that are true for you.

_____  I was given the same name as my mom or
dad and am proud to have it.

_____  I was given my name to honor my
grandparent or another family member.

**SIOK-TIN**

_____  I was named after my mom's favorite saint.

_____  My parents really loved my name and
wanted me to have it.

**Thomas**

_____  I was given the name of an outstanding
person in my community or country.

**Cleora**

# All Saints' Day

Among Catholics it has long been a custom for parents to name their children for saints. Saints are people who live outstanding lives as followers of Jesus. Saints put all their energy into doing what is good. They use the strength of their spirit to overcome what is bad or wrong.

Francis of Assisi is one saint whom we honor. He gave up money, parties, and fancy clothes. Instead he spent his time in prayer and joyful love of all God's creatures.

The Church names many people as saints. Each saint can help us learn more about how to be true

followers of Jesus. In prayer we can ask the saints for help to lead good Christian lives. We can ask in prayer for fairness to all people and for peace among people.

We celebrate the Feast of All Saints on November 1.

All holy men and women, pray for us that we may live more like Jesus. Amen.

# Advent

Are you the one who is to come, or should we look for someone else?

Based on Matthew 11:3

## Preparing Our Hearts

Advent is the first season in the church year. During Advent we get ready for Jesus to come into our lives. We prepare our hearts for Jesus by being loving and caring.

## Activity

This Advent house has windows with messages written on them. Each message tells one way we can prepare our hearts to welcome Jesus.

For each week of Advent, choose one window and follow its message.

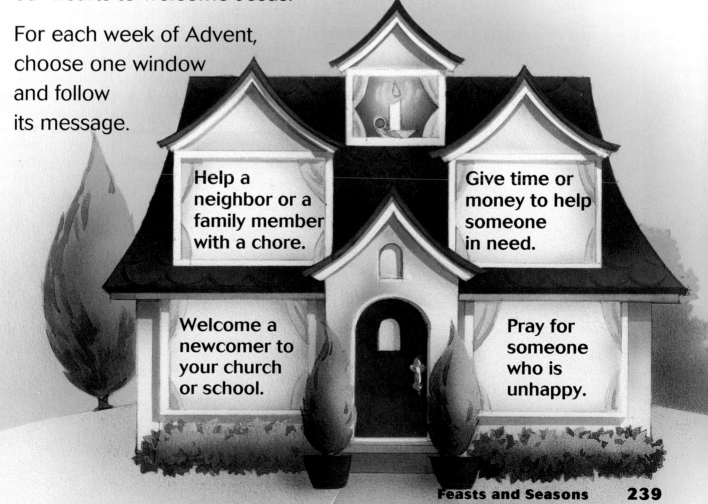

Help a neighbor or a family member with a chore.

Give time or money to help someone in need.

Welcome a newcomer to your church or school.

Pray for someone who is unhappy.

# Waiting for the Promised One

**O**ne Advent reading at Mass tells the story of John the Baptist. He was a cousin of Jesus. John preached to people in the desert. He had a special message. He said, "Make ready the way of the Lord." He wanted the people to prepare their hearts and minds for Jesus.

Based on Matthew 3:3

When Jesus began teaching, John sent messengers to ask Jesus, "Are you the one for whom the people have been waiting for thousands of years?" Jesus answered, "Tell John that the blind see, the lame walk, the deaf hear, and the poor have heard the good news."

Based on Matthew 11:2–5

Hearing these words, John knew that Jesus was the Lord. The time of waiting was over.

Lord Jesus, come and save our world today. You have done great things for us. We are filled with joy. Amen.

240

# Christmas

 The shepherds hurried to Bethlehem, where they found Mary and Joseph, and the infant Jesus.

Based on Luke 2:16

## Lighting the Way

Jerry and Manny live next door to each other. Today they had fun playing a computer game at Manny's house. When it was time to go home, Jerry saw that it was getting dark outside. His friend's mother gave him a flashlight. The light made it easier for him to see the path. Jerry was able to get home safely.

## Activity

Light makes it easier to see things. You can be a light by showing a friend how to do something like tie a knot, or by making that person happy. On each stepping stone below, write a way in which you have been a light to someone.

# The Good News of Christmas

Angels announced to shepherds that Jesus had been born in Bethlehem. This was Good News indeed! The Son of God had come into our world. Jesus was to be our light and our life.

One way we celebrate Christmas in our homes is by decorating with lights. Many families trim their Christmas trees with bright lights. Some place candles in their windows. The lights show that we are happy about Jesus' coming.

We believe that Jesus Christ is truly the Light of the World. Jesus shows us the way to bring happiness to others and to always live as holy people.

Jesus,
Light of the World,
help us to be light
for others.
Amen.

# Lent: Ash Wednesday

 Guide me in your ways, O Lord. Your path leads to your truth.

Based on Psalm 25:4–5

## Marked with Jesus' Sign

We begin Mass with the Sign of the Cross. This prayer reminds us of our faith.

The cross is an important symbol to Christians. Jesus died on a cross for our sins. We display the cross as a sign of our belief in Jesus. During Lent we think about the meaning of the cross for our lives.

## Activity

On this cross write one thing you will do for someone during Lent. Then, decorate and color the cross.

# The First Day of Lent

Ash Wednesday is the first day of Lent. On this day we gather in church and are marked with ashes. The priest or deacon dips his thumb into the ashes, then traces a cross on our foreheads. The cross of ashes means that we want to follow Jesus more closely.

Did you know that the first time you were marked with the cross was at your Baptism? Your parents and godparents marked you with the Sign of the Cross. A priest or deacon anointed your head with oil in the Sign of the Cross. At Baptism, you became a member of Jesus' community, the Catholic Church. Catholics make the Sign of the Cross to remember Jesus' love for everyone.

Jesus, we are happy to be members of your community, the Church. Help us live each day as your followers. Amen.

# Lent: Forty Days

**Have mercy on me, O God, in your goodness.**

Psalm 51:3

## Time for Prayer

During Lent, we remember how Jesus spent time in prayer. Jesus calls us to think and pray as he did.

- We pray to **ask** God to help us and others.

- We pray to **praise** God's goodness.

- We pray to **thank** God for our many blessings.

## Activity

Think about how you will pray during Lent. Complete each sentence below.

I will ask God to help me

_____

_____.

I will praise God for

_____

_____.

I will thank God for

_____

_____.

# The Forty Days of Lent

The season of Lent lasts for forty days.

Lent is a time to ask questions. We could say that Lent is an "examination of conscience" for forty days. Am I acting the way a member of Jesus' community should act? Do I show care and kindness to other people? In what ways can I be more loving to others?

During Lent we try to become better followers of Jesus. We try to show more love for other people. We do good works in the name of Jesus Christ. We pray that the Holy Spirit will help us make good choices. In doing all these things, we show our love for God and one another.

Dear Jesus, help me to choose good things to do during Lent. Amen.

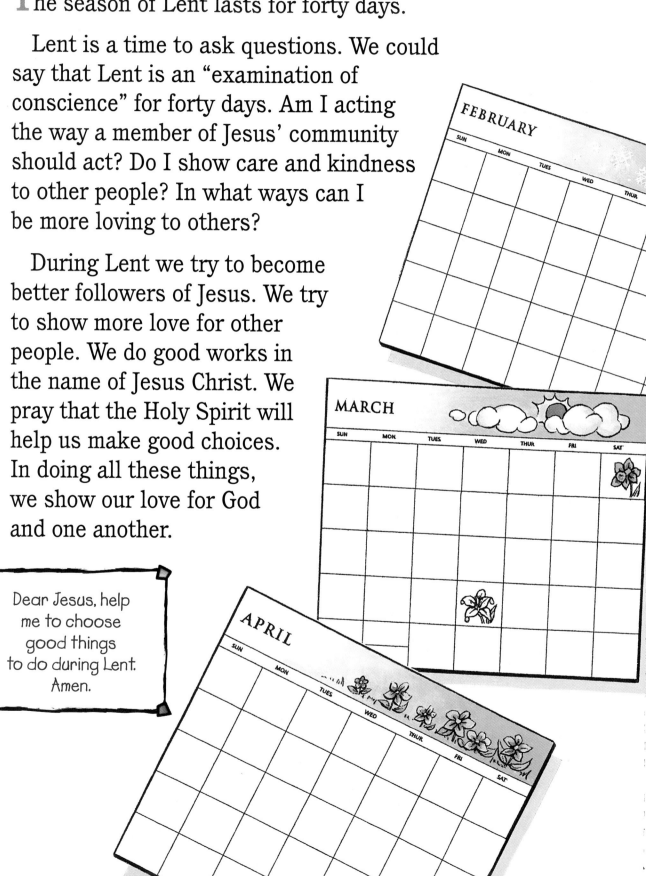

# Holy Week

 Jesus said, "Take this bread and eat it. This is my Body. I give it to you."

Based on Matthew 26:26

## Three Holy Days

**D**uring Holy Week we celebrate three very holy days. Read again Jesus' words at the top of this page. Jesus said this on Holy Thursday at the Last Supper. On Good Friday we think of Jesus dying for us. We think of new life on Holy Saturday.

## Activity

Write the correct day under each sentence.

We remember the Last Supper.

_____

- - - - - - - - - - - - - - - - - -

_____

We remember the day Jesus died on the cross.

_____

- - - - - - - - - - - - - - - - - -

_____

We celebrate Jesus' rising to new life.

_____

- - - - - - - - - - - - - - - - - -

_____

# Three Days Before Easter

**O**ur three holiest days begin on Holy Thursday evening. On Holy Thursday we remember the special meal that Jesus shared with his followers. This meal is called the Last Supper. Jesus gave his followers his Body and Blood in the Eucharist. He did this to show his love and concern for them.

Good Friday is another holy day. On Good Friday we remember the suffering and death of Jesus. We remember that Jesus died on the cross because of his love for us.

On the night of Holy Saturday we celebrate Jesus' rising to new life. At the Easter Vigil we begin our Easter celebration. We begin our new life in the Risen Christ.

Jesus,
thank you for
giving yourself to us
in the Eucharist.
Amen.

# Easter

 I have seen Jesus! He is alive!

Based on John 20:18

## Words of Joy

We can show we are happy and filled with joy in many ways. Sometimes we sing. Sometimes we dance. Sometimes we even shout and jump up and down. We might even give someone a great big hug!

We also show our joy in the words we use. These words let others know just how happy we are.

## Activity

Circle the words below that you might use to show you are filled with joy.

# Alleluia! Jesus Is Risen!

Easter is our most important feast. On Easter we celebrate the Good News that Jesus is not dead. Jesus is alive! He is with us today!

Our parish community gathers at Mass. We sing songs filled with joy. We pray prayers of thanksgiving. We thank God for giving new life to Jesus.

We say "Alleluia" to show how happy we are. Jesus has risen! Alleluia is our Easter word of joy and peace. During Lent, our church community does not sing "Alleluia." But now it is Easter, the Resurrection, our greatest feast of the church year. We pray and sing, "Alleluia." We listen to the Word of God that tells of Jesus' new life. We are happy and filled with God's joy.

Jesus,
you are risen
from the dead.
Alleluia! Alleluia!
Amen.

# Mary

Hail, Mary, full of grace. The Lord is with you.

Based on Luke 1:28

## The Hail Mary

Our Church honors the saints with our prayers. Our greatest saint is Mary. The prayer we use most often as a church community to honor Mary is the Hail Mary.

## Activity

Pray the words of the Hail Mary slowly. Fill in the missing words.

_____

Hail Mary, full of _____,

the Lord is with thee.

Blessed art thou among women,

_____

and _____ is the fruit of thy

womb, Jesus.

_____

Holy Mary, _____ of God

pray for us sinners, now

_____

and at the hour of our death. _____.

# A Prayer to Honor Mary

God's angel, Gabriel, came to Mary and said, "Hail Mary. The Lord is with you!" The angel told Mary that she would give birth to God's own Son. "The Holy Spirit and the power of the Most High will come over you." Mary loved and trusted God. She said "yes" with these words, "May it be done as you say."

Later Mary went to see Elizabeth, her cousin. Elizabeth said to Mary, "Blessed are you among women, and blessed is the fruit of your womb, Jesus."

Based on Luke 1:26–42

The words of the angel and of Elizabeth are in the Hail Mary. With this prayer we honor Mary, the Mother of God. We ask Mary to pray for us now. We ask her to pray for us always. The Hail Mary is part of another special prayer, the Rosary.

Hail Mary, we honor you as the mother of Jesus and as our mother. Pray for us. Amen.

# Saint Margaret of Scotland

**Give them something to eat.**

Based on Matthew 14:16

## Service to Others

Jesus came to teach us how to serve one another. He showed us how to help people.

## Activity

One picture shows Jesus teaching. The other shows his friends serving food to hungry people.

What did Jesus teach his friends to do?

_____

- - - - - - - - - - - - - - - - - - - - - - - - - -

_____

# Saint Margaret of Scotland

Margaret of Scotland was a queen. She was married to Malcolm, the king of Scotland. They were very rich and could have lived selfish lives. But Queen Margaret was not happy keeping all the riches for herself. So she and the king shared their money and food with the poor people of their country. They gave people in slavery their freedom. They cared for everyone who needed love.

Queen Margaret prayed every day. She read the Bible and taught her children to love God. She also taught them to care for people in need. Margaret chose to live as Jesus lived.

In time, Margaret became the patron saint of Scotland. Today we honor Saint Margaret for her service to God's people. She is a Christian hero. November 16 is the feast of Saint Margaret.

> Saint Margaret of Scotland, pray with us for all those people who are in need today. Amen.

# Holy People

See what love the Father has poured out on us.
We are called the children of God.

Based on 1 John 3:1

## Same but Different

Annie knows she looks like her mom. But Annie acts more like her dad. And in some ways, Annie is like no one else. She is special!

Michael is adopted. He doesn't look like anyone in his family. But Michael is like his family members in other ways. He is kind. He has a good sense of humor and likes to laugh.

You may or may not look like another family member. Maybe you act like your older brother or sister. Or maybe you just act like yourself. But there is one way in which you are just like everyone else. You are a child of God! And that makes you and everyone else very special!

## Activity

Complete the sentence below.

I am special because

_____

- - - - - - - - - - - - - - - - - - - - - - - - - - - - - - - - - - -

_____

_____

- - - - - - - - - - - - - - - - - - - - - - - - - - - - - - - - - - -

_____.

# Father Nelson Baker

**A**s a young man, Nelson Baker ran a successful business with a partner. But, Nelson felt that God was calling him to be a priest. In 1876, at the age of 35, he was ordained.

Soon after, Father Baker became the director of an orphanage and a school for boys in New York. The organization was very much in debt. Father Baker used his gift of business skills. He formed the Association of Our Lady of Victory. He asked members across the United States to pay dues of 25 cents a year. So many joined that he was able to pay all debts!

Father Baker also opened a home for infants and a hospital in 1911. He was called "Padre of the Poor."

Father Baker died in 1936 in the very hospital he had founded. Our Lady of Victory Hospital operated until 2002. Then the buildings were made into apartments for low income seniors. People said this was a way of continuing Father Baker's mission.

> Dear Lord, help us to follow the example of Father Baker. May we use our gifts as he did. Amen.

# Feast of Pentecost

 You will receive power when the holy Spirit comes upon you.

Acts 1:8

## Sharing Good News

Sometimes we hear more bad news than good. We need to hear and read about more good things happening in our world. Good news gives us hope. It brings us happiness and peace.

## Activity

Think about some good news you have heard. Write a headline for a story about good news.

GREAT Weather Today!

Happy Thoughts page 5

The GOOD ♥ NEWS

Sharing Joy and Love

# Come, Holy Spirit!

After his Resurrection, Jesus Christ told his followers to wait for a special promise from God. They waited in Jerusalem with Jesus' mother, Mary. Crowds of people began coming to Jerusalem. It was time for the Jewish festival of **Pentecost**. Jews had come from faraway places to worship in the Temple.

As Jesus' followers prayed together, a sound like a strong wind filled the room. Then, small flames of fire rested on each person. The Holy Spirit came to give them strength. They started telling people about Jesus. They shared the Good News with many people. The number of Jesus' followers grew and grew.

Based on Acts 2:1–47

The feast of Pentecost comes fifty days after Easter. On Pentecost, we celebrate the birthday of the Church. The Holy Spirit remains with the Church today. The Holy Spirit makes us strong, helping us to follow Jesus.

> Holy Spirit, you came to guide followers of Jesus. We ask you to help and guide us today. Amen.

# OUR CATHOLIC HERITAGE

## What Catholics Believe

## How Catholics Worship

## How Catholics Live

## How Catholics Pray

# WHAT CATHOLICS BELIEVE

*To have faith is to believe in God. We come to know God through the Bible and teachings of the Church.*

## ABOUT
# THE BIBLE

The Bible is a special book about God. Bible stories tell how God loves and cares for all people. You can learn more about the Bible on pages 17–21.

## ABOUT
# THE TRINITY

There is only one God. There are three Persons in God—the Father, the Son, and the Holy Spirit. We call the three Persons in God the **Holy Trinity.**

### God Our Father

God is our heavenly Father. He loves and cares for us. God made everything in creation with love.

### Jesus Christ

Jesus Christ is God's own Son. Jesus became a man. He died on the cross and rose from the dead for us. Jesus is our Savior. He saves us from sin.

### The Holy Spirit

The Holy Spirit is also God. We receive the Holy Spirit at Baptism. He gives us special gifts to share with others.

## ABOUT

# THE CATHOLIC CHURCH

We are Catholics. We are the People of God. As followers of Jesus we celebrate the sacraments. We share the gifts of the Holy Spirit. We pray to God in many ways. We can pray with others or by ourselves.

The Catholic Church is our faith community. Our faith community shares the Good News about Jesus. Helping and caring for others is a part of being Catholic.

## ABOUT

# MARY

God blessed Mary in a special way. God chose Mary to be the mother of Jesus. Mary loved and cared for God's Son, Jesus.

We call Mary "Mother," too. She is our mother in heaven. Like a good mother, Mary loves and cares for us. The Rosary is a special prayer to honor Mary.

Mary is our greatest saint. Saints show us how to follow Jesus.

## ABOUT

# NEW LIFE FOREVER

Jesus teaches us to act with love. When we act with love, we will be happy with God in heaven after we die. **Heaven** is happiness with God forever.

# HOW CATHOLICS WORSHIP

*Worship is giving honor, thanks, and praise to God. We worship when we pray and when we celebrate the Eucharist. We worship when we celebrate the sacraments.*

## ABOUT
# THE SACRAMENTS

Sacraments are celebrations of God's love for us. We celebrate that we share in Jesus' new life. There are seven sacraments.

**Baptism** is the sacrament that welcomes us as new members of the Church. We receive the Holy Spirit. Baptism takes away all sin. We share in the new life of Jesus.

**Confirmation** is the sacrament in which the Holy Spirit makes our faith in Jesus Christ stronger. The Holy Spirit helps us share the Good News about Jesus.

**Eucharist** is the sacrament in which we share a special meal with Jesus. The Eucharist is God's gift of love to us. When we celebrate the Eucharist at Mass, we remember the sacrifice of Jesus. We thank God for giving us the Body and Blood of Christ.

**Reconciliation** is the sacrament that celebrates the gift of God's forgiveness. It also celebrates the gift of God's love for us. We say we are sorry for our sins. We promise to turn away from sin. God shows mercy and forgives us.

**Anointing of the Sick** is a sacrament of healing. It is the sacrament of Christ's peace and forgiveness. People who are sick, elderly, or dying receive this sacrament.

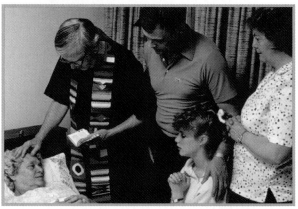

The Sacrament of **Holy Orders** celebrates priests, deacons, and bishops. These baptized men are called by God to serve others in the Church.

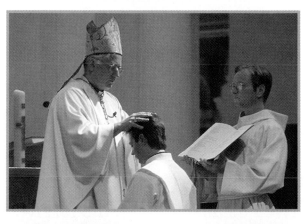

**Matrimony** is the sacrament that celebrates the love of a man and a woman for each other. A husband and wife share God's love with their children. They serve one another and the community.

# ABOUT
# RECONCILIATION

We can celebrate the Sacrament of Reconciliation with our parish community. We know that we all need God's forgiveness and mercy.

**Introductory Rites** We sing a song of praise. The priest welcomes us and prays with us.

**The Word of God** We listen to readings from the Bible. The priest helps us understand the readings.

**Examination of Conscience** We think about our words and actions. We ask the Holy Spirit to help us turn away from sin. We pray the Lord's Prayer together.

**Rite of Reconciliation** We pray a prayer of sorrow. We each go alone to confess our sins to the priest. We talk about the words or actions for which we are sorry. Then we ask for forgiveness. We receive a penance. The priest gives us absolution—the forgiveness of God.

**Proclamation of Praise** We praise and thank God. We are happy that God forgives us. We are happy that he loves us always and forever.

**Concluding Prayer of Thanksgiving** The priest offers a blessing for us. We sing a song of praise.

## Steps to Reconciliation

When we receive the Sacrament of Reconciliation we meet with the priest. We follow these steps:

1. **Examination of Conscience**
   I examine my conscience. I ask myself some important questions. Have I hurt other people or myself? Have I done hurtful things on purpose?

2. **Welcome** The priest welcomes me. I make the Sign of the Cross and say, "In the name of the Father, and of the Son, and of the Holy Spirit. Amen."

3. **Reading** The priest may read a story from the Bible. The story will be about God's love, mercy, and forgiveness.

4. **Confession of Sins** The priest listens as I talk. I explain my sins. I tell the priest how I may have hurt myself or others.

5. **Penance** The priest asks me to say a prayer or do an act of goodness. This penance will help me make up for what I have done wrong.

6. **Prayer of Sorrow**   I tell God I am sorry for my sins. I say a Prayer of Sorrow. This prayer is also called an Act of Contrition.

 page 15 for a Prayer of Sorrow.

7. **Absolution**   The priest says a prayer in the name of the Church. Then he asks God to forgive my sins. The priest gives me absolution, which is the forgiveness of God.

The priest says, "I absolve you from your sins in the name of the Father, and of the Son, and of the Holy Spirit."

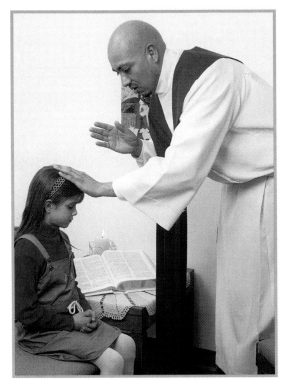

8. **Prayer of Thanksgiving and Dismissal**   With the priest, I thank God for being forgiving. This is called the Prayer of Thanksgiving. Then the priest says to me, "Go in peace."

I answer, "Amen."

## ABOUT
# THE MASS

The Mass is the best way to worship God.

1.  Our celebration begins. The priest and the other ministers walk to the altar. We stand and sing a song of welcome.

2.  We make the Sign of the Cross. The priest welcomes us with these words: "The Lord be with you." We answer, "And also with you."

3.  We remember our sins. We ask God and other people to forgive us. We then sing or say the Gloria. It is a prayer of praise and thanks.

## The Liturgy of the Word

4. We listen to the Word of God in readings from the Bible. After the first two readings we say, "Thanks be to God." We sing responses to a Bible psalm.

5. We stand to sing "Alleluia." The priest or deacon reads the Gospel story. We listen to the Good News of Jesus. We say, "Praise to you, Lord Jesus Christ."

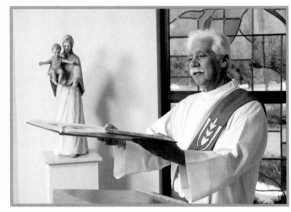

6. The priest or deacon gives a talk called a homily. It helps us understand the Bible readings.

7. We stand and pray the Nicene Creed. We say what we believe as Catholics. In the Prayer of the Faithful we ask God to help all of the People of God.

## The Liturgy of the Eucharist

8. We bring gifts of bread and wine to the altar. We prepare to share a special meal with Jesus. We remember that Jesus always loves us.

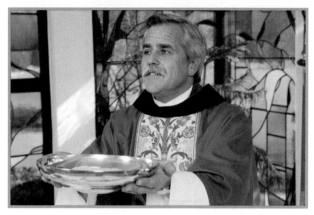

9. The priest offers our gifts of bread and wine to God. We thank and praise God for all of our blessings. We especially thank God for the gift of Jesus.

10. The priest prays as Jesus did at the Last Supper. Through the Holy Spirit bread and wine become the Body and Blood of Jesus Christ.

11. We say a prayer of faith. We may say, "Christ has died. Christ is risen. Christ will come again." The priest says a prayer to praise God. We answer, "Amen."

**12.** We pray the Lord's Prayer together. This is the prayer that Jesus taught us to say.

**13.** We offer one another a Sign of Peace. This sign reminds us to live as Jesus teaches us to live.

**14.** We receive the Body and Blood of Christ at Communion. We say, "Amen." Together we sing a communion song. We give thanks and praise for the gift of Jesus Christ in the Eucharist.

**15.** The priest gives us God's blessing. We go in peace to love and serve all people.

The Order of Mass

## HOW CATHOLICS LIVE

*God wanted to help everyone lead good lives. God gave us the Ten Commandments. Jesus teaches us how to live. Jesus gives us the Holy Spirit to help us make good choices.*

### ABOUT

# THE GREAT COMMANDMENT

The **Great Commandment** tells us how to love God and other people. Jesus said, "Love God with all your heart. Love your neighbor as yourself."

Based on Mark 12:30–31; Deuteronomy 6:5

### ABOUT

# THE NEW COMMANDMENT

Jesus gave us the **New Commandment.** He said, "Love one another as I have loved you."

Based on John 13:34

God wants us to be loving people. We show our love by caring for all living things. When we do not treat others with love, we sin. Sin is turning away from God. It is choosing to do hurtful things on purpose. The Holy Spirit helps us stay away from sin and choose what is good.

# ABOUT
# THE BEATITIUDES

The Bible tells us a story of Jesus as a great teacher. The story is called "The Sermon on the Mount" (Matthew 5:1–10). Jesus taught his followers eight Beatitudes. The Beatitudes tell us how to live.

| The Beatitudes | Living the Beatitudes |
|---|---|
| Happy are the poor in spirit. The reign of God is theirs. | We are poor in spirit when we know that we need God more than anything else. |
| Happy are the sorrowful. They will be comforted. | We try to help those who are in sorrow or those who are hurting. We know God will comfort them. |
| Happy are the gentle. They will receive all that God has promised. | We are gentle and patient with others. We believe we will share in God's promises. |
| Happy are those who hunger and thirst for justice. They will be satisfied. | We try to be fair and just toward others. We share what we have with those in need. |
| Happy are those who show mercy. They will receive mercy. | We forgive those who are unkind to us. We accept the forgiveness of others. |
| Happy are the pure of heart. They will see God. | We try to keep God first in our lives. We believe we will live forever with God. |
| Happy are the peacemakers. They will be called the children of God. | We try to bring God's peace to the world. When we live peacefully, we are known as God's children. |
| Happy are those who are treated unfairly for doing what is right. The kingdom of heaven will belong to them. | We try to do what is right even when we are teased or insulted. We believe we will be with God forever. |

# ABOUT
# THE TEN COMMANDMENTS

We can find God's commandments in the Bible
(Exodus 20:1–17). The Ten Commandments help
us know right from wrong. They are God's laws.
When we live by them, we grow in holiness.

## Living God's Laws

1. I, the Lord, am your God. You shall not have other gods beside me.

2. You shall not take the name of the Lord, your God, in vain.

3. Remember to keep holy the Sabbath day.

4. Honor your father and mother.

5. You shall not kill.

6. You shall not commit adultery.

7. You shall not steal.

8. You shall not bear false witness against your neighbor.

9. You shall not covet your neighbor's wife.

10. You shall not covet anything that belongs to your neighbor.

# ABOUT
# VOCATIONS

God calls each of us to live our lives in a special way. This is called our "vocation."

God calls some people to a religious vocation. This is a call to a special way of life in the Church. Priests, deacons, and religious sisters and brothers have a religious vocation. Priests do the work of Jesus by saying Mass, celebrating the sacraments and leading the parish community.

## Catholics can

- help at Mass by reading Scripture, leading songs, or giving Holy Communion to people.

- share the Gospel message of Jesus.

- treat all people fairly.

Some religious sisters and brothers teach. Some help the poor. Others serve as parish leaders.

Deacons serve in many ways. At Mass they can read the Gospel or give the homily. They celebrate the sacraments of Baptism and Matrimony. Deacons also help people who are in need.

As you get older, God will call you to service in your Catholic community. You might read Scripture at Mass. You might be a teacher. Perhaps God will call you to a religious vocation.

## ABOUT
# RELIGIOUS SISTERS

Religious sisters have a special vocation. They belong to groups called communities. They spend their lives working for God and for all of God's people.

Some sisters are teachers. Some sisters work with the poor, the sick, and the elderly. Still others are missionaries. They bring the Good News of the Gospel to people in countries all over the world.

Each religious sister makes important promises. She promises to love and serve God. She promises to live a simple life. She promises to be an example of what is good. And, she promises to show others how to live a good Christian life.

# HOW CATHOLICS PRAY

*Prayer is talking and listening to God. We can pray anywhere and at any time. God is everywhere. God always hears our prayers.*

## ABOUT

# KINDS OF PRAYER

When we pray, we spend time with God. We need to pray every day. Everyone can pray. There are many reasons to pray. We can pray for someone we love. We can say a prayer of sorrow to God. We can pray just to share our thoughts with God. We can say, "I love you, God." We can pray to say, "Thank you, God."

We can pray with others, as we do at Mass. We can pray by saying a prayer quietly in our hearts. We can pray by sitting very still. We can just listen to the sounds around us.

A dance, a song, and a smile can each be a prayer. If our hearts are filled with love, then our actions become special prayers.

## ABOUT
# THE LORD'S PRAYER

The Lord's Prayer is a very special prayer. It is a prayer to God, our loving Father. Jesus taught us the words to say. In this prayer we honor God. We pray that what God wants for us will be done. We ask God for what we need.

# The Lord's Prayer

Our Father who art in heaven, hallowed be thy name.

God is our Father. We praise God.
We pray that everyone will say God's name with love.

Thy kingdom come.

Jesus told us about God's kingdom. God's kingdom is happiness with God forever.
We pray that everyone in the world will know God's love.

Thy will be done on earth as it is in heaven.

We pray that everyone will live in peace. We pray that everyone will follow God's Word.

Give us this day our daily bread,

God is good. God cares for us. We pray for our needs and for the needs of others.

and forgive us our trespasses as we forgive those who trespass against us,

We ask God to forgive us when we sin. We remember that we must forgive others, too.

and lead us not into temptation,

We pray that God will help us make good choices.

but deliver us from evil.

We pray that God will protect us from things that may harm us.

Amen.

Our "Amen" says that Jesus' prayer is our prayer, too.

# Write-in Glossary

**absolution**
(page 80)

_____

- - - - - - - - - - - - - - - - - - - - - - - - - - -

_____ is the forgiveness of God given through the priest in the Sacrament of Reconciliation.

**act of contrition**
(page 101)

_____     _____

- - - - - - - - - - -     - - - - - - - - - - - - - - - - - - - - -

An _____ of _____ is a prayer that tells God we are sorry for our sins.

**Anointing of the Sick**
(page 263)

_____     _____

- - - - - - - - - - - - - - - - - - - - - - - - - - - -     - - - - - - - - - - - -

_____ of the _____ is a sacrament of healing. It brings peace and the forgiveness of Christ to people who are sick, elderly, or dying.

**Baptism**
(page 38)

_____

- - - - - - - - - - - - - - - - - - - - - - - - - - - -

In the Sacrament of _____ the Church welcomes us as new members. Baptism takes away original sin and all other sin.

**Bible**
(page 18)

_____

- - - - - - - - - - - - - - - - - - - - - - - - - -

The _____ is the written Word of God. It is also called Scripture.

**bless**
(page 227)

_____

- - - - - - - - - - - - - - - - -

To _____ means to ask for God's good will toward someone.

**blessing**
(page 227)

_____

- - - - - - - - - - - - - - - - - - - - - - - - - -

A _____ is a prayer that asks for God's gifts for others or for ourselves.

**confession**
(page 80)

_____ is telling our sins to a priest in the Sacrament of Reconciliation.

**Confirmation**
(page 262)

_____ is the sacrament in which the Holy Spirit makes our faith in Jesus Christ stronger.

**conscience**
(page 71)

Our _____ helps us know right from wrong.

**contrition**
(page 101)

_____ means to be sorry and to want to stay away from sin.

**creation**
(page 113)

God made all _____ good.

**Eucharist**
(page 165)

The _____ is a sacrifice and a special meal of thanks. We receive the Body and Blood of Christ.

**free choice**
(page 71)

_____ is the freedom God gives us to choose between right and wrong.

**Gospel**
(page 18)

The _____ is the Good News of Jesus in the Bible. The four Gospels tell the Good News of Jesus' life and teachings.

**grace**
(page 81)

The gift of _____ is God's loving presence in our lives.

**Great Commandment**
(page 271)

The _____ _____ is Jesus' teaching about how to love God, ourselves, and others.

**hallowed**
(page 185)

_____ is another word for "holy."

**heaven**
(page 261)

_____ is happiness with God forever.

**holy**
(page 49)

To be _____ means to be like God.

**Holy Communion**
(page 165)

We receive the Body and Blood of Christ in _____ _____ _____ _____.

**Holy Orders**
(page 207)

_____ _____

_____ _____ is a sacrament in which bishops, priests, and deacons are ordained to special service.

**homily**
(page 123)

_____

A _____ is a talk given by a priest or deacon. It helps us understand the Bible readings we hear at Mass.

**justice**
(page 217)

_____

_____ means to treat people fairly.

**Liturgy of the Eucharist**
(page 164)

_____ _____

The _____ of the _____ begins as we prepare to share a special meal at Mass.

**Liturgy of the Word**
(page 123)

_____ _____

The _____ of the _____ is when we listen to God's Word from the Bible at Mass.

**Lord's Prayer**
(page 185)

_____ _____

The _____ _____ is the prayer that Jesus taught us.

**Mass**
(page 29)

_____

The _____ is a special meal that Jesus shares with us. The Mass is both a sacrifice and a celebration.

**Matrimony**
(page 207)

_____ is a sacrament in which a man and woman promise to be faithful to each other for their whole lives.

**mortal sins**
(page 91)

_____ _____ are serious sins. They separate us from our friendship with God.

**New Commandment**
(page 175)

The _____ _____ from Jesus is, "Love one another as I have loved you."

**Nicene Creed**
(page 123)

Catholics tell what they believe when they pray the _____ _____ _____ _____ at Mass.

**original sin**
(page 39)

_____ _____ is the sin of the first man and woman.

**peace**
(page 217)

_____ means getting along with others.

**penance**
(page 100)

A _____ is a prayer or kind act to make up for the harm caused by sin.

**People of God**
(page 29)

The _____ of _____ are followers of Jesus Christ.

**praise**
(page 59)

_____ is a joyful type of prayer. It celebrates God's goodness.

**prayer**
(page 59)

_____ is talking to and listening to God.

**Prayer of the Faithful**
(page 143)

The _____ of the _____ is the last part of the Liturgy of the Word at Mass. During this prayer we pray for the needs of people everywhere.

**psalms**
(page 59)

_____ are prayers from the Bible that people often sing.

**Reconciliation**
(page 80)

_____ is a sacrament of healing. It celebrates God's love and forgiveness.

**Resurrection**
(page 155)

_____ is Jesus' being raised from the dead to new life.

**sacraments**
(page 39)

_____ are special signs of God's love and presence.

**sacrifice**
(page 155)

_____

- - - - - - - - - - - - - - - - - - - - - - - -

A _____ is a special gift
that is given out of love.

**saints**
(page 49)

_____

- - - - - - - - - - - - - - -

_____ are people who show great love for
other people and for God.

**Savior**
(page 155)

_____

- - - - - - - - - - - - - -

A _____ is someone who rescues others
from danger. Jesus is our Savior.

**Scripture**
(page 18)

_____

- - - - - - - - - - - - - - - - - - - - - - -

The Bible is also called _____.

**service**
(page 133)

_____

- - - - - - - - - - - - - - -

_____ means doing work that helps others.

**sin**
(page 71)

_____

- - - - - - - - - - - - - - -

To _____ is to do hurtful things on purpose.
Sin is disobeying God.

**Son of God**
(page 113)

_____    _____

- - - - - - - - - - - -    - - - - - - - - - - - -

_____ of _____ is a
special title for Jesus. Jesus is God's only Son.

**spiritual gifts**
(page 196)

_____

- - - - - - - - - - - - - - - - - - - - - -

The Holy Spirit gives us _____
_____

- - - - - - - - - - - - - - -

_____. Some of these gifts are
knowledge, wisdom, healing, and faith.

**temptation**
(page 185)

A _____ is wanting to do something that is wrong.

**Ten Commandments**
(page 90)

The _____ _____ are God's laws. They help us to know how to lead good lives.

**trespasses**
(page 185)

_____ are sins or wrongs.

**venial sins**
(page 91)

_____ _____ are less serious sins. They weaken our friendship with God.

**vocation**
(page 274)

A _____ is God's call to us to live our lives in a special way.

**Word of God**
(page 113)

The _____ of _____ is God speaking to us in Scripture.

**works of mercy**
(page 133)

The _____ of _____ tell how to take care of the needs of others.

# Index